The
IDEAL
HORSE

The
IDEAL
HORSE

A Common Sense Guide to Training for All Riders

BURT PHILLIPS

Illustrations by Jan Smith

AN ARCO EQUESTRIAN BOOK

PRENTICE HALL PRESS • NEW YORK

For my wife, María Rebeca, who tolerated me while I wrote this book, and for my children, Irving, Rose, and Noah, who will learn from it.

Published by Prentice Hall Press
A Division of Simon & Schuster, Inc.
Gulf + Western Building
One Gulf + Western Plaza
New York, NY   10023

PRENTICE HALL PRESS is a trademark of Simon & Schuster, Inc.

This book was originally published in 1982 by Exposition Press.

Library of Congress Cataloging-in-Publication Data
Phillips, Burt.
  The ideal horse.

  (An Arco equestrian book)
  Includes index.
  1. Horses—Training. I. Title. II. Series.
SF287.P47 1986   636.1'0888   86-5048
ISBN 0-668-06603-2

Manufactured in the United States of America

Designed by Stanley S. Drate/Folio Graphics Co. Inc.

10 9 8 7 6 5 4 3 2 1

First Prentice Hall Press Edition

Contents

1

About the Horse

In order to be able to work logically with a horse, one must understand how his mind works.

All horses suffer somewhat from claustrophobia (the fear of being trapped) as evidenced by nervousness in a box stall, fear of horse trailers, and bridle-fighting horses that have had their heads trapped by the bit, heavy hands, and tie-downs.

In this book I shall explain how to train a horse (teach him something new) without arousing this phobia. In the first place the horse has a marvelous memory. He never forgets. That is why first impressions are so important. If a horse has a bad first experience with a horse trailer, he will be difficult to load for life; and the same holds true for all the other things (bits, saddles, riding) to which he must become accustomed in the course of training.

A horse's ability to think/reason is directly proportionate to his degree of calmness. The more excited he becomes, the more impaired is his thinking ability; the more calm, the easier to train. A thousand pounds of bone and muscle with no controlling brain—a completely excited horse—is a dangerous animal that may destroy his rider and himself. Archaeologists claim to have found evidence of prehistoric horse herds that were excited and chased over cliffs to their death in man's ruthless hunt for meat.

And, just as a horse cannot think while excited, he also cannot learn or be trained.

1

We are all aware that a horse is capable of learning some things and not others. For example, he will never learn not to overeat grain, no matter how many times he has colic or founder, yet he will learn not to eat cactus after one attempt.

There is a simple explanation for these different learning abilities: his mind is capable only of *direct association of ideas.* He cannot reason indirectly! And as the cactus produces pain at the exact moment of biting, he learns it is the cause of the pain. The grain causes pain moments later, and he cannot connect the cause with the resulting pain.

You must keep this aspect of his learning ability in mind while training a horse. For example, a kicking horse can be retrained if his haunches are struck with a whip *while they are in the air in the act of kicking.* If the whip is applied after the rear feet land, he will be incited to kick again. Many of us have seen the rider at a horse show who takes his horse behind the barn and beats him (indirect punishment requiring indirect thinking) for having performed badly in his previous class. In such a case, the horse can only think that the rider is sadistic and enjoys inflicting pain.

Horses are gregarious; they have a strong herd instinct. They do not like to be alone and will at times fight violently to join their stablemates. In the herd, they always establish a hierarchy, a pecking order, a chain of command. When a human joins the herd, by entering into a relationship with a horse as trainer or rider even though the herd consists of one horse and one human, the horse will relate to the human as another horse, and a pecking order will be established. If the horseman does not want to be dominated by the horse, he must, from the beginning, establish himself as the herd boss. In order to do this it is necessary to understand a horse's capacities and fears.

The homing instinct still exists in the horse's brain, although it is largely forgotten and much less esteemed by today's horsemen. The old-time cowboy, who knew his mount would take him home through a blinding blizzard, regarded this ability highly.

In addition to his homing instinct, many of the horse's actions are dictated by the fact that he *does not like pain.*

I mention it because of the overwhelming evidence to the contrary. Ill-fitting, painful bits and chain curbs; saddles that are too narrow for the shoulders, or that sit down on the withers and grind and grind; dirty, too-short cinches that grind their rings and dirt into the horse's axilla (armpits); heavy leather girths that can blister in hot weather; inconsiderate, heavy-handed, unbalanced, sit-back, loin-crushing riders—all seem diabolically designed by *horse-lovers* to inflict pain and make the horse miserable. And then, in their ignorance, they say, "I don't know why this *stupid* horse won't work!"

Horses will fight or run from pain. Many a horse has been driven to temporary insanity by the nagging pain of a heavy hand or severe bit, or both. The pain builds until the animal goes mad and carries his terrified rider through a fence.

We merely need to observe the successful dairy industry to realize that animals are able to do their work better if they are comfortable, happy, and contented while they are working or resting.

Now let us consider a horse's physical potential. A mature horse has a certain body, conformation, and bone structure, decreed by his genetic pattern. Every foal carries the genetic pattern in which he will develop. Through sound nutrition and systematic gymnastic training, we can assure that he will reach his potential, but we can never improve him beyond that—we can never improve that which nature has given.

Too often you can see a stumpy-pasterned, straight-shouldered horse that someone has decided should be a jumper. The result is easily predictable: premature lameness from the jarring concussion that the stumpy front legs are unable to withstand.

Common also is the dressage horse or stock horse with weak, crooked hocks that has been forced, because of the collection required for these disciplines, to carry his weight on his rear legs. Result: bog spavin, bone spavin, and lame hocks.

Why were these horses prematurely ruined? The answer is because we tend to force our image of the type of horse we admire over the horse we own at the moment.

Let's step back and take a good look at our horse. What is his particular talent? What will his conformation allow him to do without insidiously destroying his joints? If we can answer these questions honestly, we will save the horse endless hours of pain and save ourselves from the heartbreaking lament, "I just got him trained, and he went lame!"

Just as important as conformation, and perhaps more, in judging a horse's potential, is character and disposition. If a horse is lazy, lethargic, lacking in congenital verve, his character is obvious, but his disposition may still be friendly and kind or mean and vicious.

Mean and vicious horses should be sold—eventually they will gravely injure someone. After all, we are working with horses for pleasure, not because we have a strong death wish. Those who do would be better to take up the sport of rodeo riding.

The lazy horse with a kind disposition would be best used as a child's horse, trail horse, or pleasure horse. We will be sadly disappointed if we spend many months training him for a job that requires an abundance of natural impulsion or spirit (such as dressage, reining, or gaited work and collection). Conversely, a spirited, high-strung horse is just as limited in the type of work to which he is suited.

Always try to choose the best goal for your horse logically by judiciously considering his character, disposition, and conformation.

2

Training Goals

To plan a training program successfully, we must choose an end, a goal, toward which we will work. That which we do first must be progressively directed toward that which we will be doing a week, a month, or even years in the future.

A professional knows, and keeps in mind at all times, where he is going with a horse, for he knows the impossibility of erasing his mistakes from the horse's mind. If you are not sure of the ultimate goal you have in mind for your horse, if you feel that you need more time to observe and determine your horse's particular talents, then in the meantime choose the intermediate goal of creating a pleasure horse, either English or Western.

All horses should first be trained to a pleasure horse level, and then taken on to their advanced specialties. By pleasure horse, I mean a horse that is calm and well-mannered on the ground as well as from the saddle; a horse that will walk, trot, and canter (with a fair amount of balance) and knows his leads; a horse that will obey smoothly, but slowly, the bit and cues to move forward; a horse that is dependable on those long quiet rides in the country.

A horse's training can be considered as two phases, roughly equivalent to grade school and high school. The goal of the grade school is to produce a horse that works well in natural gaits and responds obediently, but from whom we do not expect quick responses or transitions.

Most horses are endowed with a natural walk, trot, and canter, and it is in these gaits that we wish the horse to perform well, without undue force from hand or leg.

In this phase of training, we will not ask the horse to stop abruptly from the canter or trot; we will always go from the canter to the trot to the walk to the stop.

When using a snaffle bit, we can slow our horse without making him grin or move his head; accelerate (extend his stride) easily with no strength of leg and stretch him forward to the bit; do transitions from one gait to another smoothly and easily, we will know that our horse is nearly ready for the second phase of school, high school.

Unhappily, not all horses can be taken into the second level of training. If the horse has poor conformation of the hindquarters or rear legs, if he is dull and spiritless, it will be wise to end his training at the first level and not torture him with training that is beyond his capability.

In the second level, we take the horse on to collection. As much mystery exists about this term, I will take a moment to clarify its meaning: A horse that is *ready, willing,* and *able* to execute his rider's commands immediately is collected.

A standing horse, or one performing a natural walk, trot, or canter, is carrying seventy-five percent of his weight on his forelegs. Collection will shift the load further onto the rear legs by moving them closer to the front legs, a process defined by Waldemar Seunig as "evenloading," or making the horse carry his weight equally on all four legs. When a horse is in a state of collection, he is prepared for quick, powerful movements.

There is so much confusion concerning collection that the late Alois Podhajsky (former director of the Spanish Riding School), wrote in his book, *Classic Dressage,* "At the Olympic Grand Prix dressage level, it is rare to see a true collected trot." Consequently, as most of the readers will never see a horse in true collection, let's take a look at false collection—we can learn by knowing what to avoid.

A collected horse will usually have his neck arched. This shape is the root of much of the confusion about what constitutes collection. This ideal has been interpreted to mean that to collect a horse, one must cause his neck to bow—an assumption that produced a Pandora's box of apparatus: tie-downs, martingales, bitting rigs, etc.

The arched neck is the *result* of training (of pushing the rear legs closer to the front, of having the horse truly come to the bit), *not* the *cause* of it! The neck arches because the horse is collected, but the arched neck does not make the horse collected. A horse is not collected when his head is pulled down and his neck bends at the third vertebra. This only increases the load on the already overloaded forelegs. A horse in this unfortunate position is incapable of free forward movement or extension of stride; he is doomed to slowly destroy the joints of his forelegs.

A horse that will not shoot forward at the slightest cue is not collected. A horse that is heavy on the bit is not collected. A horse that is not smooth to ride, whether his gait is slow or springy, is not collected.

If one can avoid false collection, one has a chance of reaching the true end of training—collection.

3

Training Equipment

Even the greatest, most gifted trainer cannot do a proper job without at least the minimum of proper equipment, but excess is unnecessary. If you cannot train a horse with a halter and lead rope, training cavesson and two lunge lines, lungeing whip and five-foot riding whip, training snaffle bit, and a comfortable saddle—if you need a trunk full of running martingales, tie-downs, and cruel leverage bits (curbs), then you do not know how to train a horse.

As all of our steering and slowing will depend on the horse's acceptance of the bit, let's discuss the various bits available that can make, *or ruin*, a horse's mouth.

All bits are capable of producing pain in the horse's mouth, although the curb, with its crushing leverage, is undoubtedly the king in this realm.

The snaffle ranges from a very mild, thick, flexible, rubber bit to a jointed egg-butt training bit to a thin double-twisted-wire that is more suitable for grinding hamburger than for making a horse's mouth.

The egg-butt snaffle with a jointed mouthpiece of appropriate thickness (the thinner the mouthpiece, the more severe the bit), a minimum diameter of one-half inch at the thickest point, will suffice for all but the initial introductory training period with completely green mouths. During this period, there is less risk of the horse forming an aversion to the bit if the soft rubber snaffle is used.

The jointed snaffle allows the rider to apply independent pressure on either corner of the horse's mouth. It also has a nutcracker action if strongly applied. If you firmly grasp the mouthpiece in one hand and allow someone to give the reins a strong pull, you will discover that even the mild jointed snaffle is capable of producing considerable pain.

The curb bit is frequently misused. Most riders and horses using it are not ready for it—the horses have been trained to obey not the *signals* of the bit, but only the *pain* of it. The riders do not know how to teach their horse to obey bit signals and are using the crushing action of a leverage bit as an emergency brake.

After a horse is thoroughly obedient and collected in a snaffle, a mild, well-adjusted curb bit may be used successfully to increase his direct flexion and collection, refining his collection through the slower, feathering action that is possible only with a leverage bit.

When the reins of a curb bit bridle are pulled strongly, the bottom shanks move rearward and up, and the upper shanks move

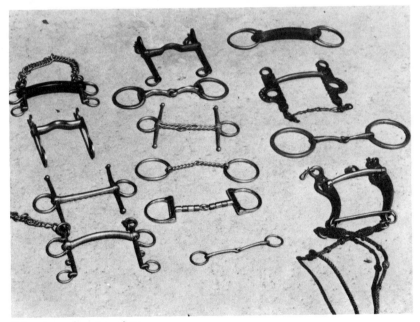

Selection of various bits

Double bridle

forward and down. This action puts a lifting pressure on the corners of the horse's mouth via the mouthpiece, and a downward pushing pressure on the poll via the headstall. This action forces the horse to bend his neck at the third cervical vertebra in false compliance to the bit. (To feel this poll pressure, place a finger between the crownpiece and the poll and apply a stopping rein action.) The curb bit must be introduced gradually in conjunction with the training snaffle—a full double bridle.

I will cover completely all that needs to be said of cruel and barbaric bits (the spade, ring, or extra-long shanked bits) with the statement: "If you are good enough to use them, you don't need them."

All aluminum bits are worthless, except possibly for nailing on the wall as bridle racks. The aluminum has an unpleasant taste that prevents a horse from ever being happy with it, and its extreme light weight gives the rider very little feel. If you slacken the reins, frequently the feather-light shanks fail to fall forward and inform the horse that he has been released.

A discussion of controlling devices would be incomplete without some words about the jáquima or as it is known in English, the hackamore.

In Europe, as early as the fifteenth century, a form of training cavesson, consisting of a *padded* metal noseband with nose and side rings and headstall was used to train horses.

The placement of the nose and side rings allowed the trainer to slowly obtain the lateral flexion so necessary to proper training.

Some years after the Spanish had arrived on the North American continent, they found themselves blessed with vast herds of cattle. As there was virtually no market for beef, the cattle were marketed as tallow and dried rawhides. Due to the scarcity of iron these were used as a substitute by the Spaniards, and the jáquima was one product of the process.

The plaited noseband (bosal) has a rasplike surface which quickly scrapes the nose and jawbone raw. Abrasion to this sensitive area allowed the early Californian to control the wild bronco *quickly*— but this is bronco busting, not horse training. A true horse trainer must always be able to say, "I have plenty of time." For when one begins to hurry (to train at *his* speed, not the *horse's*) one begins to ruin the horse.

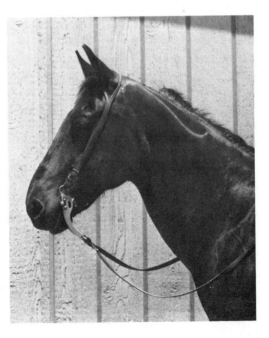

Aluminum bit stuck in pulled-back position with slack reins

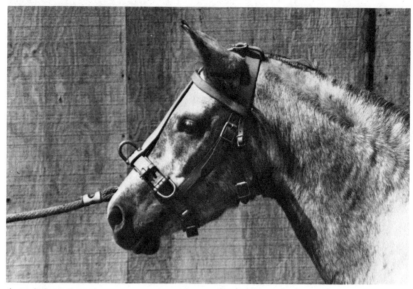

A training cavesson

The second, and greater, disadvantage of the jáquima is inherent in its structure. The bosal is knotted together under the horse's jaw, and this is the only section to which the reins may be attached. As all green horses start their training being led from the ground with a direct rein (also called a leading rein or buggy rein), and as a direct pull on the jáquima rein will twist the horse's head in the *opposite* direction to which he will turn, a wrong flexion, one that is against all the principles of horsemanship, is created.

I once mentioned this to a jáquima aficionado. He understood the logic of it and had rings plaited into the bosal similar to the side ring placement of the training cavesson. This solved the flexion problem, but still left the hard, rasplike bosal scraping off hair and leaving permanent cartilage bumps on the horse's nose. Being ingenious, he wrapped the bosal with sheepskin and had a workable training cavesson.

This seemed a rather involved way to come by an imperfect training cavesson and merely emphasized the lengths to which some people will go to resist a change of method.

The fact that the horse has no teeth between his incisors and molars allows us to use a bit in his mouth to signal him to slow down or turn. This also makes the common statement, "He grabbed the bit in his teeth and ran away!" ridiculous, although there are horses that, in an effort to find relief from a heavy hand, duck their

12

mouths back and grab the shank of the bit with their lower incisors. A properly attached lipping strap will break this habit.

If you gently look into a horse's mouth, you will see that the lips fold inwardly over the gums (bars) and that the tongue fills the gap between the lower jawbone and is usually higher than the edge of the lips.

In order for the bit to fit *comfortably*, it must have a curved mouthpiece or an open tongue port to arch over the tongue and provide contact and support equally on the lips (at the corners) and tongue.

Many curb bits have a tongue port that rotates and becomes higher as the shanks are moved rearward. This port was incorporated into the bit to relieve excessive pressure on the tongue and

Wrong flexion of
jáquima (hackamore)

Bit with tongue port and roller

prevent mouth-gaping habits. Then an ingenious fellow came along and filled the port with a roller with the excuse that his horse was nervous and needed something to play with in order to take his mind off of his troubles (take his mind off of his rider, who should be working to get his attention).

If you must have a roller in your bit, at least have it set high enough in the port so that ample tongue-relieving space is left under it.

The horse that accepts his bit lifts it with his tongue and gently lowers it while swallowing and chewing softly.

A comfortable bit must also be wide enough. Many bits are too narrow and chafe the corners of the mouth. There should be a quarter of an inch between the corners of the mouth and the sides of the bit.

A curb bit should measure at least one and three-quarter inches from the center of the curb-strap loop to the center of the mouthpiece, two inches being the ideal length for the average horse.

A properly adjusted headstall will hold the bit snugly against the corners of the mouth without making a wrinkle. If the bit is held too tightly, it will continuously apply pressure, even if the rider has slackened the reins. The horse will not know when the reins have been released and will begin to learn to ignore bit pressures.

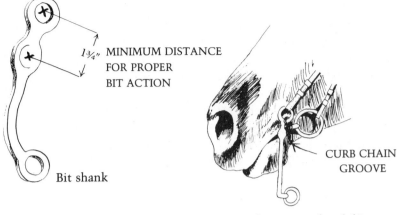

1¾" MINIMUM DISTANCE
FOR PROPER
BIT ACTION

Bit shank

CURB CHAIN
GROOVE

Correct placement of curb bit

When using the double bridle, the curb is lowered below the snaffle until it is opposite the curb chain groove. Always be sure also that the curb mouthpiece does not bounce and rattle on the tushes or incisors. It is advisable to have a veterinarian check your horse's mouth for abnormal teeth or sharp molars that will cause discomfort with normal bit placement and use.

The curb chain or strap adjustment is also critical when fitting a bridle. If it is too loose, it will pinch the corner of the horse's mouth between the curb chain and mouthpiece (*see illustration of pinching curb chain, page 236*). If it is too tightly adjusted, it will not allow the bit to rotate and raise the tongue port. Many people adjust the curb chain so tightly that the horse's tongue is under a constant pressure that prevents him from swallowing. A tight curb chain is the surest way to teach a horse the ugly habit of getting his tongue over the bit. If the shanks of the curb bit can move from where they loosely hang to no more than forty-five degrees rearward, the curb chain is properly adjusted.

Maximum bit movement allowed
by a properly adjusted curb chain

45°

Do not be confused by the "curb strap" you are likely to see on snaffle bits. It is not a curb, as it does not aid in intensifying the pressure through leverage. Its only purpose is to prevent the snaffle rings from being pulled into the horse's mouth when a strong leading rein is used.

A discussion of the curb bit is not complete without an explanation of leverage. Leverage is the mechanical application of multiplied force to an object. This force is directly proportionate to the length of the lever on each side of the fulcrum.

The principle of leverage

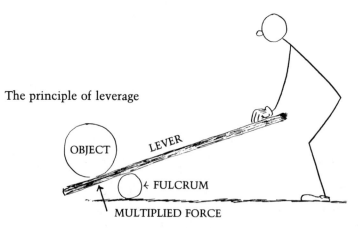

For example, a curb bit with a six-inch shank below the mouthpiece and a two-inch shank above the mouthpiece will have a mechanical advantage of three to one. In other words, for every pound of pull applied to the reins, three pounds will be applied to the mouth and the curb chain groove.

Nearly all riders can pull fifty pounds on the reins while mounted; thus they can apply a crushing 150 pounds to the horse's mouth.

As an experiment, place your finger between the curb chain and the horse's jawbone and pull on the reins. The crushing force on your finger will graphically demonstrate the action of a leverage bit.

The drop noseband, which differs from the light riding cavesson in that the strap that passes under the jaw is hinged and can drop freely, is a valuable piece of training equipment, but, unfortunately, many riders are ignorant of its function. It is often buckled tightly *below* the bit, acting like a muzzle to prevent the mouth from opening. Clearly, the rider has erroneously reasoned, "If I tie my horse's mouth shut long enough, he will learn to keep it shut and stop gaping at the mouth."

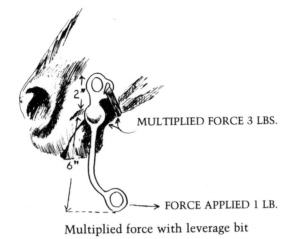

MULTIPLIED FORCE 3 LBS.

FORCE APPLIED 1 LB.

Multiplied force with leverage bit

A horse opens his mouth to escape from the pain of the bit. If he is prevented from doing this, he will move his entire muzzle back closer to his chest—and there he is, *behind the bit,* falsely collected, hollow-backed, his stride ruined.

Flexion is necessary for properly executed equestrian movements, and it starts with the relaxation of the masseter muscles in the lower jaw. But a horse cannot come to the bit with a soft chewing action if his mouth is clamped shut! The mouth must be able to open an inch or so without hindrance from the noseband.

The drop noseband should be placed *above* the bit, and the adjustable strap under the jaw should be loose (with the mouth shut) and hanging in the curb-chain groove.

I make this statement well aware that it is a common practice, perhaps even a tradition, of the majority of dressage and combined training riders to place the drop noseband below the bit in compliance with Alois Podhajsky's suggestion that ". . . the noseband, fastened under the bit, prevents the horse from opening his mouth and crossing his jaws, a bad habit often found in young horses. It also prevents the horse from yielding with the lower jaw instead of at the poll in order to evade the discomfort of bending." (*Complete Training of the Horse and Rider,* 1967.)

In answer to this, I must quote Waldemar Seunig in his book *Horsemanship* (1956): "The horse can try to evade the demands made upon it by its load, flexion, and disobedience in general in various ways. These evasions will be apparent to the casual observer in such symptoms as stiffness, false bends, *dropping the lower jaw or moving it to one side, and other vices; but the evasion of the handquarters is the primary cause of all these errors* (italics mine).

Henry Wynmalen also supports this view: "The cure usually recommended to prevent a horse from opening its mouth is to fit a drop noseband. It is a 'preventive' certainly, but it is not a 'cure'; preventing is not teaching. I see little merit in the use of the drop noseband as an aid to training apart from the fact that some of the pressure exerted by the reins may be transferred by it from the mouth to the nose." (*Dressage,* 1974.)

It is easy to see that a noseband placed low on the horse's nose will prevent the expansion of the nostrils and thereby cut down the horse's air intake, in much the same manner as the smothering bridle, which features a stiff leather noseband with padding on both sides that closes on the nostrils, used in Peru, subdues the Peruvian Paso.

The cartilage on the edges of the bony nostril openings of the skull are quite sensitive and subject to damage if excessive pressure from a noseband is placed on them. The many lumpy-nosed horses (the result of calcareous growth caused by injury to the cartilage) are evidence of a low-placed noseband.

As one can prevent excessive jaw opening by placing the noseband *above* the bit, one should not reduce a horse's air intake and cause pain or possible disfigurement by placing it below the bit.

I have trained horses to the high-school level without the use of any special type of noseband, with the snaffle bridle alone. If a horse is trained to obey his bit, to truly "come to the bit," he will not attempt evasion by excessively opening his mouth.

Years ago, it was customary to show stock horses in the American horse shows in a loosely adjusted bosalilla (a small, pencil-size bosal), as it was supposed that the horse was trained in the jáquima, and the bosalilla would be a reminder of this early training.

Soon the bosalilla was being used extremely tightly to prevent a horse that didn't obey his bit from opening his mouth. A round bosal without the customary knot under the chin was developed that could be adjusted tightly without the trouble of wrapping it.

Judges found themselves in an impossible situation: they could not see whether a horse obeyed his bit or gaped at the mouth from excessive bit pressure. As a result, a ruling was made and stock horses were not permitted to use any type of noseband while being shown.

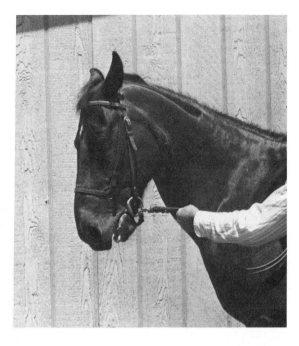

Correct action of
noseband fastened
above the bit

As soon as the dressage section of the American Horse Show Association follows this example, we will see an improvement in the dressage horses being shown in America.

To summarize the points above: when the horse's mouth opens because of a strong rein action, the lower jaw takes the slack from the noseband and transfers the bit pressure to the nose. This prevents the jaw from being opened excessively and also applies pressure to the nose that the horse can instinctively understand—and there you have the proper action of a drop noseband.

The saddle, inadvertently invented, no doubt, for the comfort of the rider, today is used by *horsemen* for the comfort of the horse.

The purpose and benefit of a saddle is to distribute the rider's weight over a larger area on the horse's sensitive back muscles. A rider astride a horse, sitting erect, sits on his ischium bones. Anyone who has held someone on his lap for any length of time will have felt these bones digging into his legs. These ischium bones pressing into the horse's muscles cause him to lower his back (become sway-backed)—the exact opposite of the goal of training: a collected horse with a *rounded* back.

It is not uncommon for a veterinarian to diagnose a sore back problem as "too much bareback riding!" At the trot, the ischium bones are merely pounded into the back muscles, but at the canter

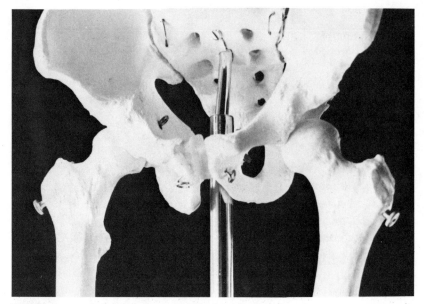

The human pelvis, showing ischium bones

they are pounded *and ground in,* and may actually wear off the horse's hair.

A strong, secure seat is a psychological advantage needed by all riders if the master-servant roles are not to be reversed and the rider find himself dominated by a willfully disobedient horse.

A bareback seat can never be as strong as a seat in the saddle, and the horse will be quick to take advantage of the rider's weakness. The stirrups, said to have been invented by the Mongolians to enhance their battle prowess, besides aiding immensely the rider's lateral balance, also increase the grip of the lower leg if it should be needed to maintain one's balance.

If a horse loses his rider a few times, he may learn that this is an excellent way to evade the rider's commands.

In addition, as a properly trained horse moves forward to an increase of leg pressure, most bareback riders cannot cue the horse, for they must *hang on* with their legs.

A horse that is properly trained to increase his forward speed in answer to a slight increase in leg pressure can be quickly untrained by the rider who merely squeezes his legs to maintain his seat and does not insist that the horse respond to the signal. As the rider doesn't realize that he has given an order, it is impossible for him to keep the horse leg-responsive.

Whenever I see a bareback rider, it passes through my mind that he is not a serious horseman (as the fact that he is depressing his horse's back and dulling his sides bothers him not at all) and is just fooling around with horses.

The top of the saddle should fit the rider's seat and legs. A saddle that is too small from front to rear will cause a rider to half stand to avoid the discomfort of being pinched, and instead of developing a deep, secure seat, he will learn to perch nervously on the horse. Or, to avoid the pain, he will push himself up the cantle in a backward-leaning, slouching, muscle-cramping position.

A saddle that is too broad across the seat will put pressure on the femur (thigh bone) below the hip joint where there is no joint, and after a few hours of riding the rider will probably develop a sore from the excessive pressure and his hip joint will feel like it is being dislocated.

A saddle that is too narrow across the seat will press between the seat bones, and one will have the feeling of being ridden out of town on a rail.

The lowest part of the seat should be in the center of the saddle seat, and should be located over the lowest part of the horse's back, immediately behind the withers. As with a sleeper sleeping in a sagging bed, the rider will always end up in the lowest part of the saddle, and on many saddles the low point is located too far to the rear and the front two-thirds of the seat built up with a hump. These saddles push the rider back and onto his tailbone, so that his balance is always behind the horse. His weight, being moved to the rear, is heavy on the horse's loin muscles and interferes with their action.

Stirrup leathers should be hung slightly ahead of the low point of the seat. If they are hung too far to the rear, the rider will be thrown forward onto his crotch and will have to arch his back excessively to maintain his balance (a hollow-backed seat).

In conjunction with the saddle that has its seat too far to the rear, one usually finds that the stirrups are hung too far to the front and lend themselves to the slouched-back-on-the-tailbone, feet-in-the-dashboard, so-called cowboy seat. I say "so-called" because I seriously doubt that a cowboy could ride a horse all day in such an uncomfortable position, and in the paintings by Charles Russell and Frederic Remington, if we are to accord them some credibility, the riders are all sitting erect, as the old "A-frame," high-cantled saddles would encourage one to sit.

Lean-back seat

Hollow-backed seat

Balanced seat on a Monty Foreman saddle

Balanced seat on a dressage saddle

The saddles that best enable a rider to sit a balanced seat are the old A-frame, slick-fork, the Cavalry McClellan, the Mexican Vaquero, the John Richard Young, the Monty Foreman forward seat, the Spanish Riding School saddle, some English saddles, and some Arabian saddles.

There is a simple test of the stirrup-seat relationship. Place the balls of your feet on the stirrup tread and stand so that your body is in a straight line and vertical (you are balanced if you are not holding yourself with your hands or gripped legs). In this balanced position, sink straight down by bending your knees (as if placing a foot on each side of a stool and squatting). When your seat meets the saddle, there should be a comfortable depression. Unfortunately, in many cases, you will find yourself sitting on a narrow raised hump in the front or middle of the seat.

It is interesting to note that no saddle trees (the carved wood that gives the saddle its strength and shape) are produced with the front half of the seat humped up. Instead, the hump is made of leather or a rounded and arched bridge of galvanized iron and nailed to the tree before being covered with leather.

I can only surmise that, with the advent of the "weekend rider," one of their number who rode seated on his tailbone, slouched back behind his horse, ordered a custom-made saddle to conform to his style of riding, and started the fad. The saddler, a man in business to make money, quickly realized the trend and produced saddles for the plethora of wrong-riding customers that quickly materialized with the sudden popularity of pleasure riding immediately after World War II.

Today, a rider who is not a complete masochist finds it impossible to sit erect in these mismade, crotch-banging saddles.

The western saddle comes with two types of horn: the low, wide horn, designed to tie a rope hard-and-fast for calf roping, and the tall, dally horn, designed to enable a dally roper (one who wraps his rope around the horn and holds one end) to stop and turn a steer on his rope at any point.

As most riders who buy western saddles have no intention of ever roping cattle, it would be a sad mistake for them to buy a saddle with a tall dally horn that would constantly be in the way of their hand on the reins.

I have often suggested (unsuccessfully) that the horn be removed, after a student, usually a small child, has been tossed forward and sat on it. The usual reply is, "No, I don't want to ruin the saddle [value under $100]. He, or she, will just have to learn not to be impaled."

I never cease to be amazed at people who will take patient care while selecting a pair of roller skates, a baseball glove, or a set of golf clubs, but when it comes to riding will grab any old saddle, throw it on a horse, and ride into the sunset with galls and saddle sores and thoroughly miserable horses.

4

Training and Retraining

First let me say that there are many young horses that have not yet been ridden who are better trained and more mannerly at what they do know (leading and lunge work, or possibly driving) than many of the older horses that have allowed riders to sit on their backs as they move about.

Having a horse *tamed* to the point where he will allow one to sit on his back while he moves about rather uninhibitedly, going when and where he chooses, has no correlation with the degree of his training.

A horse can be considered trained to a specific command only when he will faithfully and automatically respond to an order given by a trainer. He should perform calmly and willingly, with no signs of displeasure or anger, and with no *bonus* movements such as head tossing, flattening back of ears, or air biting.

The true reward for a horseman is not found in the show arena, is not a trophy of precious metal, but instead is the joy of a horse responding nicely to his commands.

We will assume that the animal you will work with is tame, as it is not the purpose of this book to instruct in the process of taming wild horses, which, basically, requires a lot of time, patience, and kind treatment.

We'll begin with the business of catching the animal and placing a halter on his head. I begin with my horses when they are born, as I wish them to think of a halter as part of their natural life.

The halter should be of flat leather, not unbreakable nylon or round rope. The unbreakable nylon halter has killed many horses, for when the horse becomes "hung up," irreparably entangled in a halter or rope, he cannot break free. The round rope is unsuitable as it cuts into the horse's flesh, cuts off circulation and causes sores. The halter need not be too strong, as we are not going to pull the animal forcefully or tie him with it.

If you have difficulty in catching the horse, merely hand-feed him tidbits for a few days (being careful to hold your hand flat to keep your fingers from being bitten), calling his name each time, and he will soon come to you. This may seem rather time consuming, but remember that we are concerned with training a horse not *rapidly*, but *correctly*.

Old "wise" horses may have to be roped for a few days before allowing themselves to be caught in a halter. Be careful not to swing the loop and scare the horse into injuring himself; merely toss it with a low swing from the ground, remembering to move slowly, keeping the horse as calm as possible.

Correct halter adjustment

Before putting on the halter, tie a lead rope ideally one half-inch of cotton eight feet long around the neck behind the ears. *Never tie a rope around a horse's neck with any knot but a bowline,* as all others will slip and choke him should he pull back (the rope rapidly sinks into the swelling neck, and it is usually necessary to cut into the flesh to free it). The neck rope will prevent the horse from learning the trick of breaking away while the halter is being put on.

Once on, the halter should be adjusted so that the noseband is just above the soft fossa, the bone channels above the nostrils.

With small foals, it is a good practice to restrain them by encircling the chest and rump with your arms. Do not squeeze, but keep the foal restrained in one spot until he calms down.

This is the best time for a foal to learn that restraint will not hurt him; on the contrary, if you stroke him and talk softly, he will learn to accept and even like restraint, and he will have come a long way in overcoming his instinctive claustrophobia.

Each time the foal struggles against your arms, restrain him (without squeezing) and say "Whoa" softly. Do not get into the habit of shouting "Ho!," as quick sharp sounds tend to excite horses, and our aim is always to calm them.

The verbal command "Whoa" has two meanings: it is an order to a stationary horse to stand still and an order to a moving horse to stop.

To teach the former to a mature horse, we will place the animal beside a fence, to prevent his turning his rump away from us, and stand on his left side with the lead rope in our left hand and a five-foot training whip in our right.

When the horse attempts to move from the spot, we tug lightly on the lead rope, being careful to keep the lead *loose,* as we are not trying to hold the horse with force but to teach him to stand quietly.

It is always advisable to apply insect repellent before each lesson, for anything that distracts the horse's attention makes the training more difficult.

If the horse tries to move back, we touch him below the hocks and repeat the command "Whoa."

With spoiled horses, it may be necessary to use something more severe on the nose. The training cavesson is ideal for this work, as the padded metal noseband is capable of delivering a decidedly painful thump.

In training a horse to stand, always start with light tugs and only gradually work up to the stronger discipline if it becomes necessary.

Beginning lungeing position

Stud chain in position

The same is true with the whip; start with a touch and work up to the painful sting that is often necessary with completely spoiled horses. Do not attempt this work with a short whip, for many a spoiled old renegade will kick at the whip before surrendering.

In this work, I have also successfully used a stud chain (used to hold stallions during breeding) woven through the halter *over* the horse's nose. Do not use a chain under the horse's jaw, as pain applied here causes a horse to throw up his head and rear. Many a handler has been injured by a rearing horse's flailing forehooves.

Within a few days, the horse will stand immobile to the "Whoa" command. It should be unnecessary to tie him while grooming him in the stall, but for a time, keep the end of the lead rope in one hand. Hold it so that the horse feels free, but with so little slack that a slight jerk can be easily given. You will know your horse is fully trained to this command, except for occasional reminders, when you can walk about the horse while holding the end of a long lead and the horse will remain standing on the spot.

No attempt should be made to prevent the horse from moving his head freely, for any attempt to trap his head will result in a head-fighting horse, and do not discipline the animal for stomping his feet to dislodge flies. Discipline him only when he attempts to move from the spot.

LEAD TRAINING

To begin, we stand our student parallel to a fence and take our position on his left, between his head and shoulder, facing the same direction as he. Our right hand will hold the lead shank about six inches behind his jaw, and our left will hold the training whip, pointed to the rear with the tip resting on the ground.

Take the slack from the lead rope with enough pressure to gain the horse's attention and to warn him that an order is coming. (Remember the rule: *Never surprise a horse.*) Next give the forward command, a clearly audible "cluck," as if sucking a hollow tooth. If the horse does not move forward, repeat the cluck and immediately *touch* him behind the hocks with the tip of the whip.

It is not our intent, at this point, to apply pain with the whip. As the horse cannot understand how we are able to touch his rear leg while standing near his head, the superior psychological advantage will be sufficient to move him forward.

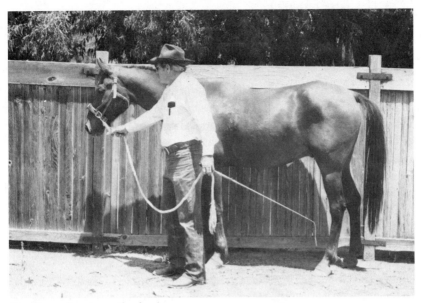
Starting a horse on the lead

As a horse does not learn words, only sounds, we will use a small number of sounds and simplify his learning task by eliminating such possibly confusing (in this context) verbal commands as "Walk" and "Whoa." As even most wild, completely untrained horses will instinctively move forward to a cluck, we will continue to use this sound as our oral forward command through all of our "grammar-school" training.

It is at this point that most students violate the basic principle of horsemanship—they attempt to pull the horse forward. The basis of all horsemanship is that the horse moves forward obediently to a command from the handler. When one pulls on a horse, the horse instinctively thinks, "You pull, I pull." And when one pulls on a human, he instinctively thinks, "You pull, I pull," and horse and handler end up in an unequal tug of war, which the larger and stronger horse must win.

Even if the horse should move forward to the pull, you are not educating him with this method, and you will find it impossible to *pull* him forward while mounted on him—unless, of course, you have extremely long arms or are using broom handles for reins.

It is well to state, at this point, that no movements executed by a horse and rider have value in themselves. The movements have value only if they exert an improving action on the horse.

For example, leading a horse forward by pulling will not improve his response to the forward command and his gradual progress from on-the-ground to mounted training.

As the horse walks forward, maintain your position between his head and shoulder and match your stride to his. Make no attempt to slow his walk, for we wish to encourage natural forward impulsion and a long stride. Maintain a light contact on the lead rope and direct the horse to the right or left by gently leading his head in either direction.

You will notice that as the horse walks, his head moves up and down and swings lightly from side to side. Your contact on the lead must not restrict this natural movement and interfere with the horse's stride. You must learn the "following hand" that is so necessary to reassure the horse.

As the horse becomes accustomed to being led properly, he will probably begin to walk slowly, with dragging steps. At this point, the trainer will be tempted to urge the horse faster by pulling forward on the lead. To succumb to this temptation would be fatal to the development of natural impulsion in the horse.

It is now time to introduce the third oral command: "Come on." This is a more difficult command for the horse to learn and thus requires more tact on the part of the trainer.

The proper response to this command is a *lengthening of stride* and, thus, a faster-moving horse—but the horse may respond by shifting into a trot. If this happens, the horse forces us to use a fourth oral command: "Easy." The horse will soon learn (as we will drag on the lead when we say "Easy") to change to a slower gait, making the transition from a trot to a walk.

It would be nice, but unrealistic, if we could use but one new command at a time, until the horse knew it well, but as the training situation changes rapidly, we must introduce the command words as they are needed. Eventually, we will find ourselves in a situation that demands that we teach the horse the second meaning of the "Whoa" command.

If when you do this you think, not of stopping, but of slowing the horse gradually until he is no longer moving forward, you will do much better at training him to stop.

While you have been walking along, your hand, in contact with the horse on the lead rope, has been following the forward movement. Now, in order to slow the horse down, at the moment of giving the "Whoa" command, your hand ceases to follow, and *you allow the horse to pull on you until he stops.*

The stop should be neither abrupt nor interminably gradual, but smooth and obedient. The horse should bring up his hind foot and "square up," not stand as if he had stopped in mid stride.

Remember that, at the moment, we are trying for correct, straight, smooth stops, and that correct, smooth, *quick* stops can be derived only from reducing the pace of the gradual stops.

Once you have undertaken this training, the horse should, in a matter of days, have learned, and learned to obey, four different sounds: "Cluck," "Come on," "Easy," and the two meanings of "Whoa."

In the case of reprimands, if one were to attempt to use a specific command for each act of the horse that displeased us, such as: "Don't kick," "Don't bite," "Don't paw," "Don't buck," etc., one would have to teach the horse so many different sounds that he would never live enough years to learn them. Instead we use a general, all-inclusive, negative command whenever the horse does something that displeases us, and, at the same moment, we make the horse uncomfortable. "No" is a poor choice of word, as the sound is easily confused with "Whoa." However, the word "Quit" works admirably as a negative command.

A word of caution: Do not make the mistake of training a horse to follow you or imitate your movements. For example, when starting forward, be sure that the horse moves first and is responding to the forward command and not merely going forward in order to follow you.

There is nothing more ridiculous (or embarrassing) than a handler who, after the veterinarian says, "Trot him out so I can see his action," trots on the spot in front of a horse, his gesture clearly saying, "Come on horse, trot like this—please!" while the horse continues to walk and stare with a puzzled expression at the antics of the unpredictable human.

When you command a horse to trot, be sure that *he* trots first!

Once the horse becomes familiar with the four basic commands while standing and leading, you can confirm and polish his responses. While the horse is standing calmly, start him in a walk with a "Cluck" and speed him up, if necessary, with a "Come on." You can also do a transition to a trot with another "Cluck," execute large circles and easy reverses with the leading rein, vary the speed at the trot with the command "Come on," and slow it by dragging lightly on the lead, do a nice transition to the walk with the "Easy" command, and come to a smooth, square stop with a gentle "Whoa," and with a second "Whoa," step back and leave the horse standing calmly. Very impressive! Your horse is now improved—and that, after all, is our goal. And you will have done it all with the same commands you will be using while mounted.

TIE TRAINING

The horses that cannot be tied, and there are many, are terribly inconvenient, for there are times when there is no one available to hold them, or no stall or holding pen in which to put them.

The horseman of the plains solved this problem by hobble-training his horse, but hobble-training, while excellent for allowing a horse to graze, will hardly keep him from wandering onto a traffic-laden street or into Grandma's tulip bed.

Many horses have been ruined for tying because their handlers violated the common sense rules for tying.

To begin with, never tie a horse to a movable object, or one that he can pull down. At first glance this rule seems fairly simple, but let me cite a couple of examples of the traps that are lurking for the naive.

A former student of mine, a serious and conscientious horse-woman, and not completely uneducated in horsemanship, for she had won the reserve jumper championship of the State of Nevada, led her thoroughbred mare up to my stable office and tied her to one of the four-by-four posts that supported the porch roof (a sturdy-looking banister connected the posts). Something frightened the mare. She pulled back, pulling the post free, with its attached lumber and projecting nails, and from under a sagging porch roof, the owner watched in horror as the mare flew down the road, the apparently sturdy hitching post banging her in the legs at each stride. A mile or so later, the mare was caught. She recovered from her injuries, but with a permanent stiffness that prevented her from jumping.

Another graphic incident happened to me while I was working my way through California Polytechnic, at San Luis Obispo, by shoeing horses. Often no one was home when I came to shoe the horses. Once, I took a horse from its stall and tied it to a handsomely constructed, strong-appearing hitch rack. The hitch rack consisted of a twenty-foot section of three-inch pipe supported by eight-by-eight posts set deeply in the ground.

Cautiously, for the horse was a stranger to me, I ran my hand down the horse's foreleg and lifted his hoof—from that moment, the action was fast! The horse exploded backward and that three-inch, twenty-foot length of pipe whisked my hat from my head like a playful summer breeze. Ducking low, for the horse swung that pipe like a flail as it spun, I ran out of range. Then a game of "catch the pipe before it hit the horse" began.

I finally grabbed the end of the pipe, and after a few minutes of "ring around the rosie," the horse stopped spinning, perhaps tired, and I untied him from the "sturdy" hitch rack. A later inspection revealed that the pipe had been secured to the posts with a metal strap and *very short nails!* A perfect trap for the unsuspecting!

Never tie a horse with a halter and lead rope that can be broken by the horse. If the horse should try to break free through fear or other reasons, and succeed, he will have learned that he *can* break free, and *he will be encouraged to try again.*

Again, this seems a simple rule to follow, but let's take a closer look at the equipment commonly in use today. With the advent of the nylon halter, most halter breakage has stopped, although on rare occasions one of the steel rings will part. The problem, the "trap," lies in the lead rope. The common lead is a half-inch, twisted, cotton rope, strong enough, when in good condition, to hold most saddle horses. The difficulty narrows down to the snap. Most of the snaps on the ready-made lead ropes are too small, and nearly any horse that strains a little can break one.

When you buy a lead rope, at the same time buy a large snap and replace the small one. The best and safest snap on the market is called the "breakaway." It can easily be released under pressure if the horse panics or becomes tangled.

Never tie a horse (à la "western movie") with the bridle reins. Not only will he break the bridle or reins if he pulls back, but he can seriously cut his mouth if the bit breaks or catches his tongue between the mouthpiece and a tooth. Many horses panic upon feeling the unyielding pull of a bit tightened through tying, thereby becoming ruined.

The United States Cavalry (mounted) had over one hundred years of horse-handling experience on which to base its procedures and it has always used either a halter and bridle or a specially constructed combination in the field.

Breakaway snap

Never tie a horse in such a way that he cannot raise his head. If his head is held down, you will awaken his claustrophobia, and in most cases he will panic.

Never tie a horse with free rope measuring more than the length of his head. He must be tied in such a way that he cannot get a foot over the rope if he should lower his head.

Unless a horse has been previously trained, you should not tie him out on a long picket rope. An untrained horse, upon tangling his legs in the rope, will panic and seriously rope burn himself. A rope burn in the area near the hooves, especially if it is on the pastern, will heal with a permanent hooflike scar that will impair the horse's action.

If you wish to "picket train" your horse, perhaps for an extended pack trip through the mountains, thread a hard-twist, half-inch rope through a thirty-foot length of plastic hose and tie a breakaway snap on each end so that the hose cannot slip back and expose the rope.

The smooth plastic will prevent the horse from burning himself if he becomes tangled. The horse must then be kept under observation for at least a week, until the trainer is sure that he will no longer "fight the rope."

There are some horses that never learn, and always throw a fit upon getting a rear leg over the rope. The cold bloods, and mustangs, with their highly developed natural intelligence, seem to be able to figure out the picket line most easily.

Unfortunately the kind of rope that is ideal for tying a horse for the first few times, without the danger of rope burns, is not available on the market. However, an excellent version can be fashioned by untwisting the three strands of a cotton rope, rolling them in balls, like yarn, and tightly rebraiding them. The resulting burn-proof rope should be at least twenty-four feet in length. If this seems like a lot of trouble just to tie-break a horse, remember that a true horseman will gladly work a couple of hours just to make his horse a little more comfortable.

A horse can be tie trained at any age, but the optimum age is weaning, or about six months.

We begin by selecting a safe place in which to tie the horse, the ideal being a head-high rope loop on a strong, smooth wall, as found in the bull pen at some training stables. There should be nothing that the horse can run against and injure himself. The ground should be soft, but with a firm footing, for if the horse should slip while pulling back, he could easily strain a muscle or ligament.

Place a well-adjusted, unbreakable halter on the horse; run a soft, braided rope through the lead ring, between the horse's forelegs, around his barrel, and tie it snugly with a bowline. *Do not use any other knot,* for only a bowline will not slip and become a hangman's knot. If you cannot tie a bowline, and cannot find a boy scout manual, or a boy scout, tie a two-inch ring in the line at the appropriate spot, using a simple overhand knot, and attach the end of the rope to the end of the ring.

Overhand knot, using
a two-inch ring in place
of a bowline

It is important that the horse *not be tied by his head,* for horses have been known to break their necks when tied for the first time.

When tied in the manner described above, the horse's head is not pulled but free to move up and down the rope. The rope only keeps him facing in one direction.

Under optimum conditions, the horse will either have learned, while yet a small foal, to be restrained without fear through having been restrained in the trainer's arms, or, if trained at a later age learned through lead and lunge training the futility of fighting a rope. Therefore, he should not panic upon discovering that he is held fast, and that the restraining rein is no longer held elastically in a considerate hand.

After a time, the horse will become bored with being restrained at the same spot and attempt to free himself. He will then learn in fact, *teach himself,* the futility of pulling against a fixed rein, a rein

Tying for the first few times

that holds fast, but never pulls or jerks in anger, an inanimate rein that has the unlimited patience that the human hand should develop. I can still hear my father, a Montanan ex-cowboy saying, "All you need to train horses, boy, is the patience, stubbornness, and brains of a post."

When the horse pulls back on the rope, it will tighten around his barrel and pull his shoulders forward, making it impossible for him to brace his forelegs and strain against the rope. Also, the squeezing of the barrel at the heart level will cause the horse to step forward instinctively. If the horse should turn and try to walk away from the spot, the rope will flex his neck and turn him back *without pulling*.

The horse should be tied for a few hours each day, thereby giving him ample opportunity to fight the rope if he is not yet completely convinced of its superiority.

To the horse, the lead rope by which he is tied *is* the rein with which he is ridden, and many runaway bit-fighting horses have been psychologically retrained by being tie trained. In much the same way, although not so brutally, as Buck learned the "Law of the Club" in Jack London's *Call of the Wild*, the horse will learn the "Law of the Rope."

5

Lungeing

When the horse is responding well to oral commands while being led, it is time to begin the next lesson—lungeing.

The saying: "Train at the trainer's speed and ruin the horse" is, and will always be, true. In fact, a horse will always tell his trainer when he is ready to advance by executing the previous lesson easily and calmly.

As with leading, we begin by placing our pupil beside a fence or wall. Stand facing the center of the horse's left side with a loose lead in the left hand and a training whip in the right, so that you can touch the horse behind and below the hocks with the whip as necessary.

Pick up the slack in the lead, making contact so as to prepare him for a command, and *cluck*. As the horse has learned to respond to this command while leading, he will walk forward. If he should refuse, again, as in leading, *touch* him behind the hocks with the whip.

Our purpose in our first lungeing lesson is merely to have the horse start, walk calmly about us on a small circle, and stop squarely.

Over the years, I have found that students tend to be over eager and try to get the horse to walk, trot, and gallop during the first lungeing lesson—consequently confusing and exciting the horse.

Lungeing is more difficult than leading, as the horse has no one to follow, so be patient and allow him to learn, for it is the horse that produces that which the trainer desires, never the trainer.

Start your lungeing lesson in the corner of a paddock, so that the two sides of the fence will help the horse to turn on half of the circle you want him to make.

Ask your horse to perform all of the stops while he is parallel to the fence and you will eliminate the tendency most horses have (perhaps they are a bit afraid of the whip) to move the rear quarters out and face the trainer. To stop the horse, increase the lunge line pressure, raise your left hand, say "Whoa," and step in front of the horse. As he becomes better trained, he will stop off of the fence equally as well as on it. If he refuses after he has definitely come to understand the command, a sharp tug on the lunge will bring him back in line.

When your horse will consistently obey the forward and stop commands, walk calmly on the small circle, stop and remain on the spot, and when the trainer has mastered the feel of increasing the pressure of ordinary contact on the line before each command and the horse's obedience has become so regular as to be a bit boring— then it is time to introduce the trot on the lunge.

To avoid undue strain on the horse's inside legs (the legs nearest the center of the circle) caused by the centrifugal force of the faster pace, he must be allowed to trot on a larger circle. The size of the circle will be determined by the size of the horse, as, obviously, a pony can trot comfortably on a smaller circle than a seventeen-hand hunter.

As long as the horse can trot fluidly and comfortably, without being pulled sideways (onto two tracks), the circle is sufficiently large.

If we continue to use the five-foot training whip on the larger circle, the horse will soon discover that we can no longer touch his rear legs and begin to disobey. So now the trainer must use a lungeing whip with a long lash. It should be a "fitting whip" in that it should fit the distance from the trainer's hand to the horse's rear legs.

It should be obvious that the trainer will be successful in direct proportion to his proficiency with his tools (whip, lead rein, etc.).

Take time to practice with the lunge whip. Try touching a fence post or a tree at a precise point, lightly, or with a bit of force.

Once you feel you have mastered this, start the horse at the walk on the small circle, feel the line, and cluck. At first the horse will probably be confused and continue to walk. Repeat the forward command and reinforce it with a touch of the whip, and, at the same time, allow the line to slip through your hand until the horse has found the circle on which he can trot comfortably.

If your horse trots forward with sufficient impulsion, you will be able to maintain contact through the line. If he trots forward excitedly, allow nature's tranquilizer (exercise of the large muscles of the body) time to take effect. If he trots lazily, giving sloppy or no contact on the line, speed up his gait with the "Come on" command and back it up with the whip if necessary.

Refrain from using the accelerating command while at the walk, as it is difficult for the horse to learn the difference between accelerating while changing gaits and accelerating while remaining *at one gait*. Therefore, wait until the horse is in a gait, such as the trot, that is more difficult to break. Early attempts at accelerating the walk invariably end with the horse changing into a foot-dragging, lazy jog-trot, or an excited, confused trot. So we delay the introduction of the acceleration command until we have the horse in a more favorable learning situation.

The trot, the backbone of training, may be defined as a two-beat gait wherein the horse jumps from one diagonal leg to the other. The diagonal leg, usually referred to as a *diagonal*, consists of a foreleg and an opposite rear leg. At a trot, these pairs of legs (diagonals) will move in exact unison.

As it is the trainer's job to improve the horse's natural gaits, he must be able to recognize the variations of the trot—not merely trot the horse any old way. Usually, an untrained horse will trot with a lazy, foot-glued-to-the-ground, toe-dragging trot, or a nervous, tense, short, choppy, hurried trot—neither is satisfactory.

We must encourage a relaxed (but not sloppy), fluid, rhythmical, unhurried trot with long strides of equal length. This will be our goal while working the horse at the trot. We will not just stand and watch our pupil choose the trot—we will choose it and polish it until it shines.

We begin by improving the transitions (walk to trot, trot to walk) until they are calm and effortless (always remembering to increase the line pressure before every command).

When we feel that the horse would do a nice, calm, obedient transition from the trot to walk if we asked for it, we can introduce the accelerating command, "Come on." If our lead training has been successful, he will extend his stride for a few steps and accelerate, at which time we must *allow the line to slip through our hand*. If the horse refuses to accelerate, repeat the command and back it up with a touch of the whip.

The horse must increase his speed, even if he breaks into a hurried trot or a gallop. Never must he be allowed to ignore the command and remain at the same pace. *The command must be continued until the horse responds.*

Of course, if the horse shoots forward into a hurried trot, it is not exactly what we want, but it is a forward response. If the horse shoots forward into a gallop, it is not exactly what we want, but it is a forward response—and that, after all, was what our command called for. Later, we will polish this crude response into the gem of acceleration that we seek.

Patience and tact are very necessary at this point, as any rough or severe punishment will tell a horse that we are *never* pleased with a gallop or an increase of speed.

If the horse accelerates into a hurried trot, allow him to trot on until he calms down, then attempt a transition to the walk. If he gallops, after three or four strides use the command, "Easy," followed by a light tug on the line, and pull him back to a trot. It is important to allow him to slow to a relaxed, normal trot of his own accord.

We make no attempt to maintain the horse at an extended, fast trot, as we are interested only in the three or four strides of acceleration. Before we ask for another acceleration, we will again execute a few trot-to-walk transitions. When the horse is calmly obedient during these slowing exercises, he will have become relaxed, and the key to proper acceleration is in having the horse relaxed before attempting it. Only the relaxed horse is capable of accelerating with an increase of stride. The nervous, tight-muscled horse, with his muscles shortened in a hypertonic condition, cannot increase his stride, even if he desires to do so.

When the horse will accelerate from a relaxed, unhurried trot by thrusting forward energetically with his rear legs, extending his head forward and down, and stretching his neck (reaching for the ground, or bit)—adding power to his relaxed muscles without stiffening and becoming choppy, then we have nearly reached our goal of adding thrust to relaxation to achieve suppleness.

It should be clearly evident that any unnecessary roughness must be avoided if the horse is not to form a nervous, stiffening reflex as he learns to obey the various commands. Herein lies the test of the trainer's skill—to teach the horse to obey calmly without the ugly bonus of fear-stiffened action.

During all of the work on the lunge line, the horse should be frequently stroked with the whip, brushing away flies when possible, to assure him that a whip is not a fearsome, hated object. He must be certain that the whip will not be used unjustly, for a horse will accept discipline if he believes it is just, but the unjustly disciplined horse will become miserable.

At this point, a most important lesson, and one that is a prerequisite for a gallop depart from the trot, should be taught: turning to the leading rein.

Although a horse learns a degree of turning while being led at the walk and trot and from trotting on a comfortable (twenty-four-foot–forty-foot radius) circle, he can learn a higher degree of turning by being gradually spiralled in toward the center, for the psychological crutch of the trainer by his side is removed. He must learn to respond solely to the leading rein.

While spiralling him in and decreasing the circle, care must be taken to prevent him from being pulled sideways into a crablike movement. He should be gently signalled to increase the angle of turn while keeping the same pace. Take care that the circle does not become too small for his ability at the moment.

In order to increase the circle to its original size, the horse must learn the command, "Get out." At the beginning, merely shaking the lunge line at his head while giving the oral command will suffice, but some horses learn to cut in through laziness or to evade contact on the lunge line.

In the latter case, the horse does not mind working on the lunge as long as he can remain free, and thus free of control. He likes this freedom from contact, for it leaves the door open for disobedience should the occasion arise.

He must be brought to hand, or the goal of eventually bringing him up to the bit in close harmony with the rider will be impossible to achieve.

With a horse that refuses to obey the "Get out" command, the lunge line must be suddenly slackened and a traveling loop thrown at the horse's head, in a motion such as is used for flipping a garden hose over a snag.

On a seriously spoiled horse, the whip may be used in an underhanded action that stings the horse in the ribs just behind the elbow, or low on the shoulder.

On thoroughly ruined stallions, and some children's horses that are spoiled to the point of being a menace, the whip must be applied vigorously across the shoulder at a forty-five degree angle from above and from the rear.

This will seem a severe method until you are faced with a horse on the lunge that charges with premeditated murder in his eye— only then will the person who believes all horses can be trained with loving kindness learn, and quickly I hope, that there are moments when self-defense necessitates strong measures.

The horse that has learned to spiral in from a circle and back out again without losing his pace has increased his natural balance and is now ready to be taught to gallop on the lunge. As with the previous exercises, the horse will tell us when he is ready to advance by executing smoothly, and certainly with no confusion or fear, that which he has previously learned.

At this point, a short discussion of the gallop (or, in its collected form, canter) is necessary.

As the gallop is a series of jumps with the front and rear pairs of legs leaping into the air separately, it would be simple to understand the choreography of the gallop if the pairs of hooves moved exactly together—but in fact one forefoot leads the other, and one rear foot leads its opposite member in the gallop sequence.

The movement is generated as follows: The horse leaps into the air, is airborne for a short time, then must land. We will choose, as our example, the left lead, remembering that we only need reverse the sequence for the right lead. In the left lead, then, the horse will land on his right rear hoof and immediately ground his left rear simultaneously with the right fore (principal diagonal). His left fore will then come down for support and he will "vault" over it into the air. We see that the gallop is a three-beat (hoof grounding sequence), four-phase gait.

The variations of the gallop are: 1) the sprinting gallop, with the front and rear pairs of legs moving exactly together with *no lead*; 2) the racing gallop, with the principal diagonal separated into two distinct beats giving a four-beat gait; 3) the lazy, slow, false, four-beat gallop, which is an impure gait and is to be avoided; 4) the disunited gallop in which the rear and forelegs are in a different lead, sometimes called cross-firing; 5) the counter-canter, in which the horse is leading with the legs on the outside of the circle (a suppling gait for advanced horses capable of a collected canter, frequently called the wrong lead or false canter in an uncollected horse); 6) and the manège canter, where the horse is cantering in place or performing a pirouette at the canter, and his inside rear hoof lands nearly an *imperceptible* split second before his outside fore hoof, the pairing member of the principal diagonal.

In order to encourage the horse into a gallop from a trot on the lunge, we increase our line pressure so as to flex the horse's head slightly toward the center of the circle and decrease the size of the circle. We then let the lunge slip and enlarge the circle. Simultaneously with stopping the steady enlargement of the circle, we "cluck." The horse, stopped from drifting out, uses his outside rear leg to stop the outward drift and shoves himself into the inside lead.

Simultaneously with stopping the increase of the circle, we give a slight lifting motion with the lunge—a signal which will become, along with the flexion, through consistent repetition, an indicator to the horse of which lead we desire.

It is not unusual for a horse to misunderstand the gallop command the first few times it is given and respond by increasing the rate of the trot. In this case, we must repeat the command, with a touch of the whip to the hocks if necessary, until he departs into a gallop. When he gallops, we must enlarge the circle to the maximum; a small circle would overload his inside rear leg or cause him to fall heavily on his inside foreleg.

At this point, we are trying for an elastic, fluid, three-beat gallop, a gallop that does not become lazy and heavy on the forehand, a gallop that does not continually break to a fast trot, a gallop that the horse will learn to maintain at a steady rhythm until he receives the "Easy" command and returns to the trot.

At the risk of being repetitious, I would remind the reader that all basic training is aimed at encouraging the horse to exactly follow his front feet with his rear feet (one track). As all four-legged animals tend to travel a little sideways (watch a dog trotting down the street), we must continually work at correcting this crooked way of traveling.

A professional trainer recognizes "crookedness" and works gradually to "straighten" his horse without letting it become a fetish that drives him to rash actions that produce a tense, nervous horse. He also realizes that crookedness is merely the result of a horse favoring the weaker of the rear legs, or inversely, loading more heavily the stronger. For horses, like people, are right- or left-handed,

First phase, posting down on right diagonal   Second phase, in flight

the more common being the right-handed with the stronger right rear limb. (This is taking into account, of course, that to compare a human to a horse, one must visualize the human as traveling on all four limbs.) Consequently, the trainer works at combating crookedness, not by pulling on the head, but with systematic gymnastic exercises that strengthen the horse's weaker rear leg and loosen his tight, stiff barrel and loins.

During the first attempts at galloping, do not gallop the horse for too long, for the inside legs will tire rapidly, and we do not wish to create an aversion to the gallop in the horse. Many horses have been taught to evade and hold back by having been worked too hard by unthinking, inconsiderate trainers.

When the horse begins to slow and gives evidence that he would like to return to the trot, a perceptive trainer gives the "Easy" command *before* the horse breaks of its own accord. If the horse breaks of his own initiative, *he must be returned to the calm trot* before being returned to the gallop. He must learn to maintain the gait until ordered to do otherwise. Anticipate the horse as the gallop falters and accelerate him, then return the horse to the trot *on command.*

If a horse switches his lead after galloping for a time, it is an indication that the legs carrying the greater weight in that lead have

Third phase, posting up on left diagonal

Teaching "get out" on the lunge

First phase, right rear in support

Third phase, vaulting over leading forefoot

Second phase, principal diagonal in support

Fourth phase, the "silent phase": in the air

grown tired. The direction and lead must be changed frequently during the initial galloping work.

In a matter of time, the horse will become accustomed to the gallop and may attempt to slow to a sloppy, heavy-on-the-forehand gallop. Each attempt in this direction must be met with a brisk acceleration that will restore the fluid elastic gait as well as reengage the rear legs under the horse.

By the use of accelerations at the proper time, the horse will soon learn to gallop slowly, but with fluid action and carriage, and so learn to move in the natural collected gallop. In departing from the trot, the lead the horse takes will be determined, as always, by the position of his legs at the moment of departure. He must be allowed to gradually learn to take each lead. One lead will always be difficult for him to learn, as it will be as though he were doing it left-handed. If he should depart in the wrong lead, make no attempt to discipline him, as he would be led to believe that galloping is an error. Allow him to gallop calmly for a time and return to the trot. When he is in a calm trot, again attempt a gallop depart with the correct lead.

During this work, the trainer-student will discover the proper time to give the gallop command so as to achieve the desired lead. The responsiveness of the horse will always determine the exact time the gallop command should be given, but with a horse that is normally responsive, the command should be given just before the forefoot that will be the leading forefoot at the gallop hits the ground.

A horse that responds sluggishly will take another step and depart on the wrong lead. A nervous horse may anticipate the command and depart early, and on the wrong lead. A precise affinity is required between the horse and trainer, a cooperation, a niceness of execution to the command, before canter departs from the trot will be well done.

I cannot stress strongly enough the importance of keeping the horse calm during these initial lead-learning canter departs.

The most obvious benefit of lungeing is that the horse receives the exercise necessary to maintain its health. But with a horseman who is interested in improving his horse, it can receive much more.

One of the most valuable benefits of lungeing, and one the horse should receive during the rest of its useful life, is that of being warmed up before carrying the rider's weight.

As a horse fresh from the stable is apt to play up and leap about, and as many owners do not have an arena in which the animal may run, it will save the horse many a pulled muscle or tendon if he can loosen up and kick out the kinks, without the weight of the rider, before being ridden. Also, psychologically, it is poor practice to fight or dampen a horse's good spirits, its desire to go forward, by riding it before it has worn off the sharp edge of its desire for action.

Teaching a horse to become habitually obedient should also be a function of lunge training. The horse and trainer will learn a mutual language, and with an understood language, confusion is eliminated.

The wise old rogue will learn that he can no longer intimidate the rider with threats of bucking or rearing. In fact, he will learn that even threats with laid-back ears and bared teeth will be met with a fearless sting of the whip on the heels, and he will discover that threatening his handler is a losing proposition, so he will soon lose the habit.

The question—one that not enough horse owners ask themselves—"What can my horse do?" will have gained many more satisfying answers by the time the horse is lunge trained. When he has finished lunge training he can respond to the forward command. His walk can be regulated until it is energetic, with the long, roomy strides of the true, free walk. A nice, smooth stop from the walk is easy, as are all the transitions between the three gaits. He will extend his stride nicely on command and reach for the bit (stretch forward). He is pleasant to be around, as he is mannerly in that he will stand on the spot when so commanded. He knows his leads and will flex his body to the arc of the circle he is following.

When you can answer your question with these answers, your hard work on the lunge will have been amply rewarded.

6

Driving

Driving in long reins has an advantage over lungeing in that we can do the following: control both sides of the horse; move on straight lines and teach the horse to turn and flex to each changed direction; control the horse from behind, similar to the way in which we can control him while riding; see the horse's lateral legs in line and strive toward having the rear hooves follow exactly the front hooves; leave the school arena and reward our pupil with long walks on a loose rein.

Driving, we have much more power over the horse through the reins than we have while riding, due to the fact that, while mounted, we have no reference to the earth and are merely pulling the horse's head toward his back while being carried along with him.

While driving, we need merely slow or stop our forward movement, with no backward motion of the hands, and we become a very heavy anchor that will eventually stop any inveterate bit-puller or runaway.

When we start driving a horse we will proceed as with an untrained horse, unless our animal is one that has been ridden for years and is being retrained. He *may* not require the same amount of work, but if you are not sure to what your horse is accustomed, it is a good practice to follow the same procedure as with an untrained horse. The difference is that a trained horse will usually go through the various stages much more rapidly but sometimes you discover that the older, well-ridden horse is terrified at, for example, the long reins dangling above his hocks. By going through green-horse training procedures, we discover which parts of our horse's necessary training have been skipped.

We begin driving by introducing the surcingle to our pupil, always observing the rule: introduce new objects or movements near the end of the lesson, while the horse is relatively tired and less apt to bolt from fear.

The surcingle is a wide band, made from varying materials (leather, canvas webbing, etc.) that is placed around the horse's barrel behind the withers, passing under the horse in the sternal groove (the shallow groove over the ribs). It should have side rings attached at the proper height to accommodate the driving reins effectively.

When first putting a surcingle on the horse, slowly allow the animal to study and smell this new object. When he is familiar with it, slowly slip it over his back, reach under his barrel, pull up the end, and buckle it *snugly, not tightly*. Many horses have been made permanently cinch-bound by unnecessary tightening of the surcingle (or cinch) the first few times. A cinch-bound horse is one who has had the cinch tightened excessively the first time it was put on him. Feeling he couldn't breathe, he panicked and threw himself over

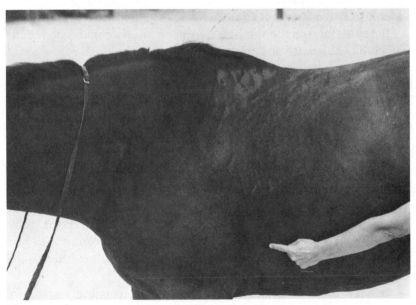

The sternal groove

Surcingle with reins at proper level

backward in an instinctive attempt to break the crushing grip of whatever was squeezing him.

With the surcingle in place, continue to lunge the horse, being careful *not to allow him to buck.*

It is instinctive for the horse to buck from pressure about his barrel, but he must learn never to buck while saddled! A few sharp jerks on the lunge will discourage this instinctive bucking, and he will soon associate bucking while saddled (in this case the surcingle acts as a saddle) with discomfort. It will become possible, as the horse slowly becomes accustomed to the pressure, to tighten the surcingle more snugly, *but it should never be tight,* as it will be only supporting the weight of the reins.

For the first few days, keep the surcingle buckled on the horse for increasing periods during the last half of the schooling period.

As soon as our pupil is accustomed to working with a surcingle, we will, at the end of the schooling period, attach a second lunge rein to the inside surcingle ring. We will now be lungeing with two reins, one attached to the training cavesson and one attached to the inside surcingle ring.

In a few days, when the horse has calmly accepted this new rein, we will cross the surcingle rein over the horse's back and attach it

Second rein attachment

Second rein crossing back

Second rein over the hocks and attached to the surcingle

to the outside surcingle ring. When the horse becomes accustomed to the rein in this position, we will slip it over his rump, so that it rides above his hocks, and continue to lunge him.

It is when the rein is in this position that the horse is most likely to become frightened and attempt to bolt or kick. By pulling him into a tight circle and striving for a calm walk until he finds that the new object is harmless, we will slowly create a calm horse who accepts the rein bouncing on his hocks.

In a matter of days, when the horse calmly accepts the rein in this position at all three gaits, we will run the outside rein through the corresponding surcingle ring and attach it to the outside cavesson side ring.

The low driving ring is sewn too close to the surcingle to permit any rein drawn through it to be used as a leading rein. It pulls too aggressively and directly toward the rear, and while a trained horse has come to accept a pull of this kind from being ridden, a green horse knows only that his head is being pulled toward his chest. He will instinctively pull back to free his head, and could develop into a head fighter.

To prevent this from occurring, a double leather strap, one foot in length, with a ring large enough to smoothly accommodate the rein, must be buckled on to the surcingle ring. This strap and ring will

Outside rein attached to cavesson

allow the reins to swing out and become truly a leading rein, although, during the first few days of training the horse to change
direction in hand it is better to leave the reins out of the surcingle
side rings and be able to immediately return to a previous lungeing
position should he develop any nervousness or confusion.

Once the leather strap has been attached, we continue to lunge
the horse, making sure that the outside driving rein does not tighten
and rise under the horse's tail, at which there might be a sudden
burst of action; that the rein does not drag the ground so that the
horse steps on it, or over it, with a rear foot; and that the rein does
not put an uncomfortable pressure on the horse's head.

It is at this point that the trainer must develop the capacity to
think with both hands simultaneously. Many students, when beginning to drive, instinctively feel that they must begin by pulling
on the reins—but quite the opposite is the case. Initially, driving is
nothing more than lungeing from behind and with two reins. The
horse will still be controlled by voice commands and by the leading
rein, as he was on the lunge. A gradual increase of pressure on the
reins before each transition will accustom the horse—eventually the
voice command will become unnecessary, and slowing and stopping
can be accomplished with just a touch of the rein. This will put the
horse more in hand, and he will also have formed the habit of yield-

Driving with reins free of surcingle rings

Driving with reins in swing-out rings

Driver accompanying horse on the circle

ing imperceptibly to the bit while answering to the forward command. The contact of a following hand will make him feel secure.

After the horse has learned to accept the rein in the new position while going through his paces on the lunge—this might take only a few days, or a few weeks, the trainer's tact and feel will tell him when the horse is ready—the trainer can start to lunge at a walk on a small circle. The difference is that now he will accompany the horse walking to one side and slightly behind him.

Gradually, over several days, he will drop back more and more until he is nearly behind the horse, then he will stop the horse and move to his other side, a stationary change of the hand, before continuing at a walk on the new circle. When this is accomplished, he will stop the horse and put him away on a pleasant note.

In time, when our pupil calmly accepts a stationary change in hand, we will attempt a change of hand at the walk, as follows.

While driving the horse on a straight line from the left side, we will smoothly cross over the line of travel behind the horse and continue on, making no attempt to turn, now driving from the right. When we reach the fence, and the horse realizes that he must either stop or turn, we will make a *gentle* right turn. In these first turns, we will return to the lungeing position and make the turn *exactly as in lungeing.*

As the days pass, we will be able to move more to the rear, continuing to change sides and make wide turns, until we can drive the horse and make gradual turns from directly behind.

The most serious difficulty encountered during the initial driving stage is in maintaining forward impulsion (the desire of the horse to move forward energetically). A horse, in some respects, is like a boat in that if it hasn't sufficient "way on" (forward movement), it will not answer to the helm.

A proper turn can be easily executed, if the horse is walking along energetically, by merely ceasing to follow the forward motion with one hand. With a lazy, foot-dragging horse, one can attempt to turn only by pulling him about, and then he will probably turn completely about and face the driver!

Remember that all movements requested of a horse have boundaries within which the careful trainer must remain. In the case of driving, the boundaries are that the horse retain its forward impulsion; that he remains on one track (rear hooves following exactly the fore hooves); that his head can move in the gently swaying, rising and falling motion of the free walk; and that we remember that even the weight and cold friction of a loose, long rein is a *heavy hand* on the head of our pupil. If we remember these ideals, we will be advancing steadily toward our goal of having a calm, well-trained horse.

TROTTING—TRANSITION WHILE DRIVING

The first attempt at trotting in the long reins will usually frighten the horse. He will hear the driver running behind and think that he is being chased. Therefore, it is best to trot the first time in a small arena, or if none is available, trot toward a corner, so that the fence can stop the frightened horse and we can avoid strong use of the reins.

Our horse will soon accept trotting in the long reins if we remember to use a very light contact that does not restrict free head movement.

At this critical moment, the horse can easily learn to be a headfighter if his claustrophobic instinct is aroused by a heavy hand. If he starts pulling on the rein, he is saying: "Do not trap my head! I can't stand it!" A wise teacher always listens to his pupil.

Make no attempt to slow down the trot. We do not wish to discourage the horse's natural ground-covering impulsion. Initially, the horse will trot faster than one wishes, but eventually he will relax and return to a calm natural trot with the steady rhythm, the only trot wherein the horse's muscles are relaxed enough for proper flexion on turns.

CROOKEDNESS

"Ride your horse forward and hold it straight!" is a famous statement at the top of the best book ever written on horsemanship, *Gymnasium of the Horse,* by Gustav Steinbrecht, a book that may be regarded as our equestrian bible. The motto, "Calm, Forward, Straight" was used by the famous French general, Alexis-François L'Hotte (1825–1904) in his book *Questions Equestres.*

Both men were world leaders in the art of equitation.

And on a less grand scale, "A horse must follow his head," was the byword of Jack Baker, past winner of the National Stock Horse Championship.

And overheard after a fall in the jumping stadium, "He wasn't watching his fence!"

Almost all horses before training, when standing, walking, trotting, or galloping will maintain a curved longitudinal flexion to the right or left; their backbones will be slightly curved in one direction, and the distance between the hip and shoulder will be greater on one side.

The rare horse that is the exception to this rule is the one in ten thousand that is truly ambidextrous. But we cannot wait for this rare exception—we must work with the average horse.

Why does a horse go crooked before training? This has been a controversial subject in the horse world for many years. Some have theorized that it is due to the fact that the foal was carried in the mare in a curved position.

This theory is disproved by the fact that dogs and other animals who give birth in multiples are crooked, and they are carried in a myriad of positions in their mothers.

Another theory is that the horse wishes to protect its hip while passing close to a wall or fence. This theory is easily disproved by the fact that crookedness does not disappear when the horse is ridden where there are no fences or walls. Also, the visible evidence of horses with knocked down hips tells us that the horse does not worry about scraping his hindquarters once his head and shoulders are past an obstacle.

The only theory that stands up is that the horse is born right- or left-handed, the more common characteristic being right-handedness.

At first, this seems confusing because the majority of horses turn and flex more easily to the left and prefer their left lead.

However, in order to explain this we need only think of the right-handed boxers who always lead with the left hand, keeping their more powerful right hand, *backed by their stronger right leg,* in reserve for the knockout punch.

With this in mind, we can readily see that a horse that is crooked to the left (bent throughout his body to the left) prefers to turn in that direction while using his more powerful right rear leg as the major propelling organ. This preference (purely mental with a new-born foal) causes one side to become gradually stronger as the animal matures.

Shoving off with the stronger right rear leg naturally flexes and turns the horse to the other weaker left leg, and the muscles on the right side grow longer, while the muscles on the left, from lack of stretch, grow shorter.

From this spring such terms as "constrained side" (shortened muscles) and "difficult side" (difficult to obtain flexions, leads, turning, etc.), for the horse feels a clumsy left-handedness while working to that side, while the muscles on the opposite constrained (shortened) side will not *stretch* and allow him to flex in that direction.

Crookedness exists, and a true horseman must learn to recognize it or join the ranks of the "crooked little riders on their crooked little horses" who think that everything is "just dandy."

A wise trainer recognizes crookedness but *does not* attempt to cure it by forcefully pulling his horse to the difficult side. Realizing that the cause of the crookedness is the weaker rear leg and failure of proper engagement of the stronger rear leg, he works at systematically strengthening the weaker leg while simultaneously holding the rein on the difficult side and allowing the horse to *gradually* stretch the constrained side as the stronger leg is engaged further. This lifts the horse's weight from the shoulder and the bit on the constrained side. This work must be done *in a time span that allows the horse the necessary time* to learn to execute left-handed movement. An excellent rule to follow is: Work the horse sixty percent on the difficult side, forty percent on the constrained side.

In this manner, we can train our pupil to be a truly two-sided horse, and thus a straight one.

Many spoiled horses have learned to use crookedness against the rider.

A professional knows that before a horse bolts, rears, or bucks, he will first assume a stiff, crooked-to-the-constrained-side posture. Thus warned, he has time to move quickly and prevent dangerous (to the horse) actions.

For a more detailed example, let us take the case of a horse that has been trained to come to the bit and is straight, but who has learned that he can successfully evade some riders, through crookedness. First he comes up to the bit evenly on both sides of his mouth, giving the rider a nice, soft, compliant feel in each hand, but after a few minutes at a working trot, he decides that the work is too hard and attempts to evade even loading (engagement) of his rear legs.

Feeling out his rider, looking for weaknesses or ignorance, he goes crooked to the left by increasing the bit pressure on the right rein, shifting his weight from the left rear leg to the stronger right rear leg, which stiffens and ceases to engage, and, by holding his neck curved to the left side, overloading his left foreleg, falls, consequently, more heavily on the forehand.

A novice rider, feeling the rein suddenly go heavy and dead in his right hand, increases his hold automatically and encourages the horse to lay on the bit on the right. His actions tell the horse that he has a green rider aboard, and he is encouraged to exploit him until, in time, the roles of rider-boss, horse-servant are reversed. The degree to which a horse will exploit the rider depends on the character and disposition of the horse.

Crookedness encourages the horse to go heavy on the forehand, and true collection, lightening the load on the forehand, is therefore impossible with a crooked horse.

As a rule a straight horse is one that is longitudinally flexed to the path he is following (his backbone is circumscribed to his line of travel, as a railroad train follows the tracks—you might think of his vertebrae as the cars and his hooves as the wheels on the tracks). But this definition suffices only for the horse moving with natural gaits, for with these he has lateral, even loading of the legs (the legs on each side are equally sharing the load) and the front pairs of legs are still carrying more than an equal share of the load.

When we have shifted the load to the rear pair of legs through collection and there is *an equal share of the load on each leg,* then the horse may be said to be straight regardless of its flexion.

When the horse calmly accepts trotting in the long reins, we can begin trotting around the arena, making easy corners with a long radius, trying for a slight bit of flexion, and keeping the rear hooves tracking the fore hooves.

At this time, we can also try to eliminate a horse's ugly habit of going from the trot to the walk with a complete lack of impulsion, falling on the forehand, and going from the trot to a foot-dragging *creep.* The horse that responds nicely to the command, "Come on" will have little trouble learning to go from the trot to an energetic walk.

A horse's education in the long reins is complete when he will easily stand on a free rein; remain standing calmly, but attentively, while the reins are picked up and contact is made; move *straight* forward, without flinching and without a slight movement to either side, with his head and vertebrae in a straight line; walk with an energetic roomy stride, keeping contact on the driver's hands through his impulsion; make a nice transition to the trot and trot calmly with a steady rhythm; change to the walk without losing his impulsion or going crooked; make simple turns while remaining on one track and without over-flexing; go from the driving position to the lunge circle and return to the driving position with no loss of timing; and, finally, come to a stop through the walk, straight and smoothly enough so that his legs are allowed to *square up* and he is not left standing in mid-stride; and do all this with just a touch of the reins.

7

Introducing the Bit and Saddle

The first bit you use on a horse should be a flexible rubber snaffle with two and a half to three inch rings. It should be wide enough to allow a quarter of an inch clearance between the end knobs or the rings, depending on the shape of the mouthpiece, and the corners of the horse's mouth. The cavesson must be fitted with rings for attachment of the bit by C snaps or straps.

The procedure for putting the bit in the mouth is as follows: Place the cavesson on the horse and leave the noseband loosened. Hand feed the horse grain or tidbits so that he is expecting pleasant-tasting morsels to be put in his mouth from the trainer's hand. Attach the bit, previously smeared with honey or molasses, to the right side of the cavesson with the bit snap. Place your right hand over the horse's nose above the nostrils, to prevent him from raising his muzzle, and slip your right thumb into his mouth at the corner. Vibrate your thumb on his tongue, and when he opens his mouth, slip in the bit with the left hand and snap it on the left with the bit snap.

Give the horse a free head so that he can chew the bit and become accustomed to it.

Follow this procedure for the next few days and you will produce a horse that will welcome the bit for the rest of his life (or at least until someone jerks a metal bit against his teeth, or pinches his

Cavesson with bit attached

mouth with an ill-made bit). After the horse has stopped chewing and mouthing the bit, tighten the noseband and lunge and drive as usual.

Do not attach the reins to the bit rings as the time is not yet ripe.

With a properly adjusted bit and cavesson, there will be enough bit movement through the cavesson to gently introduce the horse to control through the bit.

The bit must be adjusted so that it touches the corners of the mouth without causing a wrinkle. Be sure that there is ample room between the mouthpiece of the bit and the lower edge of the cavesson so that there is no possibility of the corners of the mouth being pinched.

Attach the bit to the cavesson in such a way that it will be pressed lightly against the roof of the mouth, so that it will prevent the horse from forming the ugly habit of getting his tongue over the bit.

To remove the bit, loosen the noseband, unsnap the bit on the left, place your right hand over the horse's nose above the nostrils, and gently allow him to spit it out. If he should clamp shut his mouth, insert your thumb in the corner of his mouth and rub his tongue until he chews.

Introducing the bit in this way associates bits with a pleasant taste and a complete lack of discomfort in the horse's mind.

A wise horseman will continue to hand-feed a tidbit just prior to inserting the bit to reinforce the "bit/good-things-to-eat" idea firmly in the horse's mind.

We should now continue training using the cavesson rings, allowing the horse to very gradually associate the slight bit movement with the stronger, already learned, signals of the cavesson.

If we attempt to use the bit to control too soon, we ruin the horse's mouth, for a horse has no instinct to yield to a pressure on his tongue and the corners of his mouth. All of his responses and yielding to the bit must be learned.

For example, if we place a bit in an untrained horse's mouth and apply pressure, he will feel pain and violently throw up his head, possibly rearing, and strike with a fore hoof at the bit, much the same reaction as if he had stuck his nose in a bear trap.

Whereas, if we apply hand pressure on the bridge of an untrained horse's nose, he will instinctively yield his head and possibly back up a step to relieve himself of the pressure.

The erroneous thinking that ruins many a mouth is, "I have seen horses responding to bits all of my life (especially on TV and in the movies), so they must automatically respond to a bit."

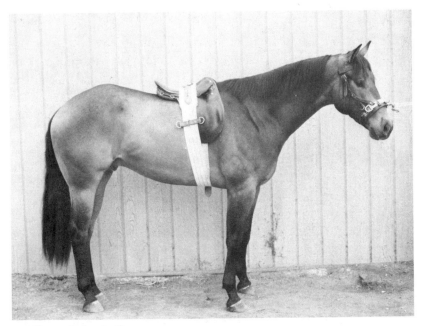

Saddle with surcingle

Remember the "Sunday rider" who puts his silver-mounted curb bit on his trusting, green, four-year-old, mounts, pulls on the reins, and says, "Back!" and realizes his stupidity as the horse rears up and over backward, just before the lights go out.

Of course, not to leave a cliff hanger, he has plenty of time to think about his mistake while lying in traction.

INTRODUCING THE SADDLE

If an old saddle is available (the one I have been using to train colts since 1946 has been fallen on, rolled on, kicked and chewed, and nothing short of an inveterate leather-eater will be able to hurt it), hang it in the horse's stall for a few days and let him learn that it is harmless. The things that a horse learns by himself, using his own natural intelligence, are the things that he learns best.

If you are using a fairly new saddle, place it where your horse can investigate—but keep watch, as he may try to eat it.

After the horse is accustomed to the smell and looks of a saddle, near the end of a vigorous schooling session carry the saddle to the horse and allow him to smell it.

When his sense of smell has assured him that it is a familiar object, although it now seems to move with a life of its own, hand-feed him grain over the seat, allowing him to eat some of the fallen grain from the saddle. While he is contentedly chewing, slip the saddle slowly onto his back and secure it snugly with the cinch or girth. The moment before the cinch is secured is a crucial one, as the horse may jump and learn that he can lose the saddle when he wishes. Try to make this moment quick, but without moving jerkily.

During the first few saddlings, do not use a saddle pad; it is unnecessary at this point and may fall and scare the horse. In this respect, it is also wise to remove the stirrups. With the saddle in place, slip a surcingle over the saddle in a way that will secure the saddle flaps and the rear of the saddle.

Now lead the horse, being vigilant to prevent any bolting or bucking by turning the horse in a tight, extremely flexed circle.

If the horse accepts the saddle calmly, but has a tight convulsive hump in his back, continue leading him at a walk until his back relaxes.

When the horse walks calmly, stops, starts, and turns obediently, as if the saddle were not there, unsaddle him and put him away, allowing him all night alone in the calm security of his stall to think about and accept this new development.

As with the first use of the surcingle, in the days following use the saddle for longer periods in the later part of the training session until the horse gradually becomes accustomed to carrying the saddle for the whole session.

Be particularly vigilant during departs into the trot and gallop, as the horse's instinct to rid its back of the uncomfortable load will be most highly aroused at this time. If he attempts to buck, a few sharp tugs on the reins and the negative command "Quit!" should discourage him.

While we are getting our horse to mentally accept the saddle, we are also strengthening his legs and muscles through its added weight (it is better to start with a light saddle). This weight is gradually preparing him for the first mounting.

8

Mounting

During all of our previous work, we frequently stood by the horse's side with our arm over his back, patting his right side with our hand, in an attempt to accustom him to the right leg that will eventually hang there. In addition to this, at times we leaned heavily upon him while stroking his neck or hand-feeding him. After he was accustomed to the saddle, we gently vibrated it and weighted the stirrups with our hands.

Now that our horse accepts these movements, there are only two more things that may scare him into a panic when he is first mounted. The first of these is the sight of the rider's body, when mounted, high above and behind him, in a very threatening position. The horse can be gradually accustomed to this sight by parking him beside a five-foot fence on which quietly sits an adult. Also, *ponying* him (leading him while on another horse), first in the arena and then on long walks in the country, will help accustom him to seeing the rider above his head.

The second of the two developments that might frighten him is the actual weight of the rider on the horse's sensitive back muscles, muscles that can instinctively cramp and cause the horse to buck or bolt and possibly learn to throw the rider, or worse, cause him to injure his relatively weak legs.

Realizing this problem, we will use the lightest person available for the first mountings.

Before attempting to mount, we will work our pupil longer than usual so that he is visibly tired. We then lead him to the fence where our rider sits. While hand-feeding him, we have the person on the fence gently slip onto his back and sit with most of his weight on the horse's shoulders.

From the beginning, and for quite some time, the *crotch-relief seat*, in which the pelvis is pushed forward, must be used, for the back of a green horse is weak, and any attempt to sit normally will cause unnecessary pain and the resulting dislike of carrying the rider.

As the ischium bones (seat bones) are shaped like sled runners, we can rock backward or forward on them, thus moving our weight respectively.

To assume the crotch-relief seat, we merely rock to the forward edge of our seat bones and lift (relieve) the weight of our buttocks from the horse's back.

Gradually, through gymnastic training, the horse's back, loin, and rear legs will strengthen, and we will be able to take the normal seat without causing the back to sag or the rear legs to drag behind in an effort to evade the painful burden.

While rocked forward on our crotch, we will carry more weight on our stirrups, our knees, and the inside of our thighs, and thus assume a *light* seat that is easy on the horse.

Regretfully, an inconsiderate rider often mounts for the first time and plops himself heavily on the saddle. Pain in the horse's tender back muscles causes them to spasm, and the horse, in an instinctive effort to dislodge the pain, bucks. If he throws the rider, he learns a lesson better left unlearned. If the rider stays aboard, the horse will very likely bow a tendon or strain a ligament or muscle. If the rider is very lucky and none of these drastic things happens, he has, at the very least, taught the horse that being mounted is a fearful, unpleasant experience.

During the first mounting, nothing traumatic or reminiscent of the Wild West should occur. Mounting should be just one more *calm* step forward in the horse's training.

After the horse has accepted the presence of the rider sitting lightly on his back, the trainer, vigilantly holding the lead to keep the horse calmly in hand, leads the horse forward four or five steps and stops. The rider dismounts on the left side, slowly, using the stirrup, and the horse is put away.

There are, of course, many different methods of mounting a horse for the first time. As long as they do not violate the principles of horsemanship, *calm, forward, and straight,* they are acceptable and may produce good results. I have merely described one that works nicely.

But there are also poor methods. For example, let me describe a method I used when I was very young, and of course, ignorant.

I had just purchased two young mares at a public auction. They were completely wild and untouched. In an attempt to calm one in the loading chute, I laid my hand on her shoulder. She trembled violently and nipped at my hand, much the way a wild fox or rabbit might do when trapped.

While hauling them home, loose in a horse truck, I decided to name the smaller mare Thunder, as she resembled Red Ryder's horse in the popular comic strip. The other mare I named Dusty for her dusty black color.

At home, I backed into the gate to the breaking corral and lowered the ramp. In no way could I chase those mares from the truck. Either they were terrified of the ramp or they chose to remain in the only place of security they had found in a mad world.

I proceeded to plant a heavy snubbing post a few yards before the loading ramp. I then roped Thunder and dragged her, inch by inch, down the ramp, where she immediately went into a wall-eyed fit, fighting the strangling noose about her neck.

When she choked down (passed out from lack of oxygen), I loosened the rope so she could breathe. In seconds, she jumped to her feet and stood staring, wise enough not to fight the rope.

Managing, somehow, to avoid her flashing forehooves, I put on the saddle and bridle, threw off the rope, wrapped her around me by the cheek strap (a method called *cheeking* by the old bronc buster) and stepped into the saddle. She exploded toward the sun like a rocket, reached her apogee, did a quarter roll, and fell. I beat her to the ground, narrowly missing the corner of the steel water trough, and she landed on her side, in a cloud of dust beside me.

Recovering first, I climbed into the saddle while she rose; then the fun began. She rushed toward the fence in a series of long crow hops, with the intention of jumping. I loosened in the saddle in preparation of a wreck. At the last moment, she changed her mind and tried to stop and turn. The result was inevitable: she fell. I stepped to the ground and mounted as she rose.

She repeated the run and fall routine three more times. I think she would have quit then, but at that moment Dusty decided to join the fun and jumped from the truck. She ran wildly about, nickering, exciting Thunder to more wild flights.

Thunder ran and fell eight more times before she stopped long enough for me to cheek her and leap off. The friend who had been standing by, in case medical assistance was needed, rushed up and asked me if I was all right. I couldn't say a word; it was a spring day in the desert near Palm Springs, and the thermometer stood at 114°.

Feeling that there must be a better way, I spent two months slowly gentling and training Dusty. Thunder developed into an undependable mount that would buck at the slightest provocation, while Dusty became a gentle, dependable horse.

If this method of "training" seems barbaric (and it is), remember that it was the method used in the days of the Old West, when a horse could be had free, or for five dollars, and was not worth the time or trouble to train correctly. My father, an old time Montana cowboy, taught me the "proper" way to train a wild one, and perhaps this fact and my ignorance of a better method can excuse my cruel and barbaric treatment of a wild horse thirty years ago.

To return to mounting; the second day of mounting should be a repetition of the first, with the addition of mounting several times, with the stirrup, after stepping down.

You will prevent the horse from forming the unpleasant habit of swinging its hindquarters away from the rider if the mounting and dismounting are done with the horse's off side (right side) next to a fence.

In the following days, have the horse carry the rider for gradually longer periods until he can make several circuits of the arena. As soon as he has developed the strength and ability to balance the weight of the rider at a walk, he must be led at a trot on straight lines, returning to the walk on the easy turns.

9
Riding the Trot

If we sat down on the horse when we first began to work at the trot, our weight, which increases greatly due to the rise and fall of the trot, would prove to be injurious to the horse's unstrengthened back and joints. The crotch-relief seat, which sufficed at the walk, is now unsatisfactory for preserving the natural position of the horse's back.

The solution to this problem is simple: the rider takes hold of the mane, or a wide neck strap provided for this purpose, stands up, leaning forward like a jockey, and uses his knees to absorb the jar of his weight. The knees will maintain the rider's balance, so his weight is not thrown from side to side on the diagonals.

As the horse slowly becomes stronger, the rider may begin to post at the trot. Posting is a combination of sitting and standing the trot in rhythm with the two-beat movement. The rider allows the thrust of a diagonal, say the right diagonal (consisting of the right foreleg and the left rear) to lift him into the air (to a standing position). He remains standing while the left diagonal (left fore and right rear) are grounded in support, then falls back (sits) into the saddle as the original right diagonal again comes into play. In effect, he is rising as the right diagonal swings forward and sitting as it swings back in support (*see photos of posting positions, pages 46–47*).

There are many advantages to posting. First, and probably the most important, is the fact that one diagonal (half the horse, in a diagonal way of thinking) may be rested, or inversely, one diagonal

74

may be given more weight in order to gymnastically strengthen a weak leg. Many years ago, the cavalry proved that a horse ridden at a posting trot can travel nearly twice as far as a horse ridden at a sitting trot. Second, the rider can evade the jar of the stiff trot and, in so doing, maintain a soft, supple seat that will aid in eventually teaching the horse a smooth springy trot that the rider can sit to comfortably.

With an untrained horse the horse usually jumps into a trot and as he comes down the weight of the rider immediately overloads his weak back and hock joints. In an effort to keep the pain from his joints, he stiffens his back while simultaneously shortening his stride and stiffening his rear legs.

This stiff, short action jars the rider's spine and causes him to stiffen his back. The rider's stiff back (now like a block of wood) falls on the horse's back, causing more pain and discomfort, and the horse stiffens his back and leg joints more, and the vicious cycle continues, ad nauseam.

An older horse who has been mistrained stiffens his stride before the pain is produced. All his steps will be short and stiff, except possibly at the walk, where he will sag on loosened joints.

This stiff, choppy gait is a contributing factor to the premature lameness of many horses. The jarring concussion insidiously produces the myriad of arthritic conditions found in the lower legs of mature horses.

The choice of which diagonal to rise on is determined by various factors. While traveling on straight lines, the choice will be governed by which legs the rider wishes to strengthen or supple; or possibly the rider will wish to alternate his weight from one diagonal to the other on a long ride.

On curved lines, it is best to load the outside rear leg and inside foreleg of green horses, for the centrifugal force of the curve places a heavier load on the inside rear leg (as the curve is the arc of a circle, the inside refers to the side nearest the center of the circle) which in the young horse has not yet been strengthened by training. It is also best to avoid any but the easiest curves.

On the more advanced horse, one whose carrying capacity of the rear legs has been strengthened by engagement, it will aid in his training and the further strengthening of his inside rear leg if we load it (post) while taking a curve.

There are two schools of thought to consider before choosing the diagonal while riding a hunt or jump course on slippery ground.

When a horse slips on a curve, he throws his head to the outside, thus changing his flexion and placing his weight on his inside rear leg. If the rider's weight while posting comes down in the saddle at this moment, it will help stabilize this leg and prevent a fall. In addition, if the rider is posting with the inside rear leg and the outside fore, his weight will cause the outside foreleg to slip first, and therefore the horse will be able to catch himself with his unburdened inside foreleg, which is in the air at the moment he is most likely to slip.

All of the riders I have observed, myself included, in this precarious position have an instinctive knowledge of which diagonal they are loading, trusting to "feel" to instinctively place their weight on the correct legs for the maximum stability.

As always, the choice of diagonal will be determined by the rider's tact, consideration, and purpose and intent of the moment. But he must intelligently choose the diagonal and not be ignorant of which leg he is loading.

While riding in a show arena, it is presumed that the horse is sufficiently advanced as to be able to carry the rider on its strengthened inside rear leg (outside fore, inside rear), and as, supposedly, the riding ring was a circle that was later extended with long straight sides, it is expected that the rider will rise and fall with the outside foreleg in preparation for the turns at the corners, although in terms of the standards of absolute horsemanship, the rider may correctly choose either diagonal on a straight track. This standard was established to aid the judge in evaluating the rider's knowledge of diagonals and general riding ability.

During a reverse of direction at the trot, the rider is expected to change his diagonal. This is easily accomplished by remaining seated for one extra trot-beat and then rising—in effect, skipping one trot-beat precisely when the direction is changed. Invariably, beginners change their diagonal by standing for an extra beat, but this is a poor practice, as the rider then misses the important lesson that posting teaches, that of feeling, through the seat, the grounding of the horse's feet. A standing change is also a detrimental habit to form in view of the fact that the rider needs his seat in the saddle at the instant he changes flexion and direction in order to make the change with firm control of hand, seat, and leg. Also, the rider is less stable while standing, and should the horse shy at this moment, he is more likely to be unseated or pull harshly on the reins to maintain his balance.

An advanced rider must know, without conscious thought, when each hoof is grounded during all movements, otherwise he would not know the precise moment to apply his controls.

Once the horse is advanced enough to work at a trot, we should advance to this gait at an early stage in a training session as it is at this gait that the horse always has two legs in support and is, therefore, more able to carry the weight of the rider.

The exact moment the horse has gained the necessary strength to withstand the increased load created by having to bear the weight of the rider will be determined by the eye and judgment of the trainer.

If the trainer is premature, he will stretch the ligaments that hold the joints tightly together and produce a loose-jointed horse, thus destroying forever the brilliant action that might have been. If he is patient, knowing that the only true progress is that determined by the horse, he will take longer, but he will finish with a nicely trained, sound, strong horse. The apparently fast method of training a horse at the trot unfortunately, is doomed from the start and will never reach this goal.

In a matter of weeks, the control must be shifted from the center of the lungeing circle (the person doing the lungeing) to the horse's back. At this time, the trainer takes the place of the mounted assistant so that the same voice and hand continues to control him, therefore eliminating the resulting confusion of change and the tension it would produce.

After a few circles at the walk and trot, the circle may be enlarged, at a walk, until the horse is moving around the perimeter of the arena.

When the horse has satisfied his curiosity by looking closely at objects that now seem threatening, for there is no one walking with him (he will soon grow confident under the calm, reassuring hand of the trainer), his work may be continued at the trot.

10

Work at the Trot

As the trot is the gait at which our horse can carry the rider's weight with less effort or damage to his joints, as it has an inherent natural impulsion that is lacking in the walk, as its simple two-beat rhythm and natural stability make it easier for the horse and rider to establish a mutual balance and cooperating rhythm, and as the horse's feet are grounded for a shorter time, making it harder for the horse to resist, it has become the backbone of training.

We are now at the stage of training when our hero (the young horse) is beginning to carry the rider at a posting trot around the perimeter of the arena. (Most horses are trained first to the left, then to the right.)

The rider prudently chooses to weight (post) the left-diagonal (left front, right rear) as he does not wish to add the last straw to the inside rear leg that will be already overloaded by centrifugal force on turns through the corners.

The young horse will tire rapidly, so he must be trotted for relatively short periods until he gradually strengthens. Never should he be ridden until he is visibly tired, for now, when he is weak, his impulsion, his spirit to go forward, can be easily ruined, forever, by overwork.

Keep the horse fresh; never let him think of his daily work as drudgery. The trainer's goal is to produce a horse that looks forward willingly to being ridden.

I anticipate that some readers of the "Work the hell out of 'em" school may take a tongue-in-cheek attitude to this, so let me cite an example:

While working as manager and trainer at San Simeon Stables for William Randolph Hearst, I frequently rode an imported Arabian stallion by the name of Zamal. His stall was at the rear of a long barn approximately seventy-five yards from the doors to the veterinarian, feed, and tack rooms in the front.

In the course of a day's work, I opened and closed the veterinarian and feed room door many times in complete tranquility. But when I quietly opened the tack room door, Zamal immediately began trumpeting and kicking the walls, sounding like an iron-booted bear in a boiler.

With the stall arrangement, it was impossible for Zamal to see which door I opened; he had the sounds completely memorized.

As I approached his stall with my saddle, the noise progressively diminished.

I opened his stall, and there he stood like a bluish alabaster statue, frozen in place, eyes sparkling in anticipation, waiting for the saddle.

After quickly saddling and bridling, I led him outside, where he stood quietly, except for an occasional slight quiver, while I mounted and settled in the saddle.

He managed to contain himself until I legged him forward, then he exploded in a series of buck jumps, bursting with sheer exuberance, around the three barns, but always moving fluidly, easy to ride. It usually took two or three circuits before he would calm enough to come out of the air and disdainfully agree to walk on the earth.

Zamal was living proof that horses can be trained to like their work.

In the beginning, at the trot, the rider will have to go faster than he wishes in order to keep the horse from falling heavily on his joints. If allowed to do so, as soon as he relaxes he will try to adopt a slow, sloppy jog/trot.

As *muscle tone* is the only thing that keeps a horse from landing heavily on his joints, we must not allow the sloppy, foot-dragging, jog/trot that will produce a ruined, loose-jointed horse.

The subject of how to train a horse to travel slowly at the trot and gallop is probably one of the most misunderstood in horsemanship.

Let me cite two comparative examples:

A novice acquires a horse that he trail rides for a time. Accidentally, usually through riding companions, he is exposed to a horse show. The desire to compete is born, and he studies the horses in the ring. It is clear that all he must do is train his horse to travel calmly, *slowly*, with a bowed neck, and take both leads at the gallop.

He starts to work to prepare his horse for a show. When mounted, he reins the horse in artifically, thus killing his natural impulse and encouraging laziness until he has destroyed the fluid action of the ordinary trot and gallop, producing a sluggish disintegrated trot which he calls a jog, and a false, four-beat canter.

While dismounted, he places the horse in the stall with his head tied in toward his chest cruelly tight, hoping as in the "shape the wet wood" method, that it will stay that way. He merely produces a behind the bit horse that cannot take a long stride, and one who bends his neck further when the reins are pulled, instead of slowing his foot action.

The big day comes. In the show ring, his horse's performance is flawless. He goes slowly, takes both leads, performs exactly as the loudspeaker directs—but he is not called out for a ribbon. Disgusted, the rider goes home muttering, "It must have been the fancy silver-mounted saddles that beat me—either that or the judge is in the horse trainer clique and is playing favorites."

The ironic point of the story is that he will at times win ribbons on his mistrained horse, because some judges have no more idea of a well-made horse than a Martian, or the judge's choice is between a "charge the bit," wild-eyed, over-excited horse or his.

If he goes to the trouble to ask the judge, "What did I do wrong?", the judge, not having the time, or feeling that he was hired to judge a show, not give a riding lesson, may merely reply, "I didn't like your horse." Or, more often, as most judges like to help novices, he will try to explain in a few words (horse show judges are extremely busy until the show ends) that the horse is not collected, is "behind the bit," "hollow backed," and "heavy on the forehand": all of which leaves our young novice just as bewildered as before.

In comparison, a professional takes a horse to train, knowing what he must do. He fully realizes that he must keep the gaits rather fast and vigorous and preserve the action, gradually slowing the trot and canter, but slowing them by keeping and increasing the action and brilliant flowing motion, keeping the rhythm of the more extended gaits and slowing the forward rate until the horse is able to take the softly collected trot and canter. And he knows that to allow the horse to disintegrate into the sloppy, foot-dragging gaits will destroy any chance he may have in the show ring. He knows full well that, at times, he will be made to appear foolish when an ignorant judge places a mistrained horse over his, but he also knows that, in the long run, he will win more than his share of the ribbons without having caused a good horse's premature lameness.

Perhaps these two examples are sufficient to explain why we must keep our young horse trotting forward vigorously with impulsion.

Our first goal at trotting will be to gradually strengthen the horse until he rediscovers the poise of the natural trot with the added weight of the rider. Necessarily, much of the natural impulsion of a highly spirited horse must be left dormant at the beginning in order to achieve a degree of relaxation and the resultant unconstrained trot. If this seems contradictory, it simply means that we must relax a horse, but not to the point of sloppy, dragging gaits. In other words, relax the horse—but not too much!

Many trainers use the term "relaxed gaits," but this term is not sufficiently specific. A better term is unconstrained (lack of mental and physical constraint or tenseness).

MUSCULAR MOVEMENT

As all work and movement of a horse is done through muscular activity, a certain degree of understanding of this phenomenon is necessary.

All muscles move the corresponding limb to which they are attached by contraction via a tendon across a joint. There are no muscles that push by extension. The extension period of a muscle is merely a passive relaxation to the contraction of the opposing muscle.

To take a step, the horse must flex (contract) one set of locomotive muscles, while at the same moment the opposing set of muscles must extend (relax). Continuous movement is a rhythmic flexing and extension of muscles, a pulsation.

The impulse for all muscular movement originates in the brain as a voluntary or involuntary action. Proof of this is demonstrated by the fact that if the spinal nerve trunk is severed at the base of the brain, all movement ceases.

If the horse is mentally constrained by fear, emotional excitement, disobedience, laziness, or confusion, his muscles will not be able to extend fully (relax), thus his steps will be short and choppy. It will be physically impossible for him to take a normal stride.

In this hypertonic, or constrained, state, in which the muscles are tense, they will be prevented from performing their important job of pumping the blood back to the heart and lungs where it will be reoxygenated.

The muscular pulsation, besides driving the horse forward, presses, during the contraction phase, on the veins, which may be thought of as tubes with check valves that do not allow the blood to travel away from the heart; thus the pulsating muscle acts as a pump through its flexing and relaxing pulsations. When this pump action is impaired by constrained muscular action, the horse will tire rapidly for want of oxygen to the muscles.

The horse will also tire more rapidly as he must, while in a constrained state, take many more steps to cover a given distance.

11

Pressure Controls: Forward, Restraining, Steering

The unconstrained trot is the basis for all further training, and a gait to which we will return whenever the horse becomes excited in subsequent training. Our immediate work at the trot will be directed toward achieving a high degree of freedom.

The horse must be responsive to three controls (forward, restraining, and steering) in order to reach this goal.

The horse has learned, in his previous schooling, to respond to these controls, but the oral forward commands we have previously used to implement them ("Cluck" and "Come on") cannot be graduated finely enough for this work. So we introduce, through a period of transition, the weight and leg forward control.

This control is taught as follows: The rider, sitting erect, picks up the reins, which are attached to the side rings on the cavesson, and makes contact with the horse's head—and with the horse's mind! After waiting for a few seconds, so that the horse does not develop the "bit-contact-go-forward" anticipatory habit, the rider rocks to the forward edge of his seat bones, tipping the pelvis forward ahead of the shoulders, a weight control that the horse feels as the weight is shifted forward on his back, relieving his loin muscles and rear legs.

Simultaneously, while rocking forward, the rider's weight presses down his heels. Now, keeping his heels depressed, the rider presses the horse's flanks with the calves of his legs and gives the oral command ("Cluck") to move forward.

After an initial period of transition, the rider will discover that the oral command is no longer necessary, except during moments of confusion and excitement, when he will, of course, resort to the combined oral, leg, and weight commands. Instead a forward control combining weight and leg will gradually be substituted for the oral accelerating command.

Now the horse's forward motion can be elicited with a degree of control that parallels the control of an automobile, with even the slightest of accelerations being obtained through the foot throttle.

A word of caution: Once the horse is moving forward at the desired rate, the leg pressure must be discontinued and a balanced crotch-relief seat assumed. Failure to do so will deaden the horse to the leg and result in an opposite response to that desired by the rider.

When used with the posting trot, the accelerating control through

Opening rein

the leg must be applied as a pulsation each time the rider returns to the saddle.

The steering will be accomplished through well-rounded corners of the arena with the opening rein—the hand moved to the side sufficiently to eliminate backward pull.

The requirements for obedience to the opening rein will be met if the horse makes the easy turns without losing rhythm of stride and does not stiffen his neck.

The restraining rein, probably the most difficult to master, must always be thought of as a slowing, not a *stopping* rein! One never stops a horse, one always gradually slows a horse until he is no longer going forward.

A relatively quick stop is in fact a long slow stop (the horse remaining supple and accepting the bit), gradually made shorter until a soft, on-the-haunches, one stride stop is possible at the trot or canter.

The long sliding-stop from a full gallop of a stock or reining horse is the one exception and is the stop of a highly trained specialist that is completely collected and finely tuned to the rider. This stop is so difficult to achieve that it is rarely seen executed flawlessly. Usually, the horse's head will be jerked momentarily straight up by the sudden, severe action of a curb bit, a fault that seems to be overlooked by many stock horse judges. It is a severe fault, as it demonstrates that the horse is stopping from pain and not from obedience to a soft, painless signal.

Strictly speaking, even this stop, *when correctly done,* is not a true exception to the rule as it is developed through the long slow stop also, the difference being that it is continued to the highest level of performance.

So, whether we slow our green horse a little or continue to a full stop depends merely on how long we continue the slowing control.

At this point, not to shatter the euphoric feeling that most horsemanship books impart that said action will always result in the proper *angelic response* by the horse, it must be admitted that not all horses will obey the restraining action of the bit.

In order to arm the reader with the necessary ability to overcome a bit-disobedient horse, we must suggest a lateral displacement action of the reins, doing so with some trepidation, knowing that some inconsiderate novice will probably ruin a good horse by *overdoing it.* Our conscience, however, is somewhat salved by the knowledge that he would probably ruin his horse anyway.

12

Turn on the Forehand

A stationary turn on the forehand (front legs) is a movement wherein the horse moves his haunches (rear legs) in a circle (or arc of a circle) about his forelegs, which move on the spot.

With the training cavesson in place, we begin this training dismounted as follows: Stand facing the horse's left shoulder, left hand holding the left rein a foot or so from the cavesson. Pick up contact on the rein and flex the horse's neck slightly to the left. Now place your open right hand on the horse's barrel (a point a few inches to the rear of the calf position of the leg when mounted) and apply a gentle pressure while simultaneously saying, "Get over."

If the horse takes one step sideways with the rear legs, immediately reward him by stroking his neck or feeding grain. If the horse does not take one step sideways with the rear legs, increase the flexion of the neck, using it as a lever against the haunches, until the rear legs step sideways one step, then immediately release the rein and remove the right hand from the horse's side, forcing a lateral displacement of the haunches.

Repeat the procedure until the horse takes one step sideways with each rear leg solely from the right hand pressure and the oral command, without increased neck flexion. When the horse responds, stop the lessons for the day. Repeat the lessons for five or ten minutes each day until the horse is responding well, then go through the training procedure on the right side.

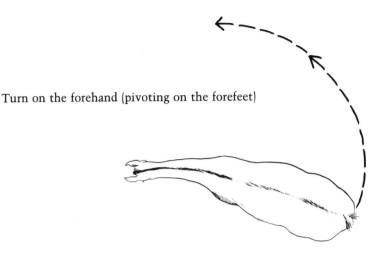

Turn on the forehand (pivoting on the forefeet)

There are some problems frequently encountered in this lesson. For example, occasionally we find a horse, of any age, that has not learned, through leading and lungeing, to flex his neck obediently. This horse must first be taught *stationary flexion* to the leading rein. We begin this lesson standing by the horse's neck, holding the left rein, with the fence at the horse's right side. Apply a gentle but positive rein pressure so as to signal the horse to bend his neck to the left. If he refuses or stiffens his neck in resistance, forcefully, with a strong pull, bend his neck to the left and immediately release the rein pressure. Repeat the lesson until the horse will easily flex his neck without moving from the spot. When the horse responds obediently to the flexing signal on the left, teach him the flexing lesson on the right side.

During turns on the forehand, some horses attempt to walk forward when the hand pressure is applied to their sides. They may be prevented from doing so by a strong holding action of the reins while maintaining the flexion. They must be prevented from walking forward, for they are confusing a lateral command (pressure on one side) with a forward command (pressure on both sides).

Occasionally, I have had students that became overzealous and attempted to speed the learning process with a sharp slap on the belly, or a stroke of the whip. This is a grave error, as, although it will produce a horse that moves laterally to a pressure signal, it also produces a horse that tightens fearfully (becomes tense) each time the control is applied. Attempts to teach this lesson with spur pricks while mounted result in the same undesirable bonuses—laid back ears and a violently swishing tail, in addition to a nervously excited, ratty horse.

Some students have difficulty in maneuvering the reins laterally, and merely lead the horse's front feet from the spot by using a forced leading rein. Once the initial neck flexion is obtained, it must be increased toward the horse's shoulder so that it works as a lever against the haunches.

There are also students who tend to blur the flexing hand on the rein and the hand pressure signal on the barrel and never obtain the perfect isolated response to the pure, lateral moving, side pressure control. In other words, they fudge with the rein hand, unconsciously, and the horse learns to move his haunches to the side to the flexing rein (an undesirable response)—proving that any lesson when done a little wrong (without feel), can prove more injurious than beneficial.

Finally, there are students who try to squeeze the first side step from the horse by shoving strongly on the barrel with the right hand. This is a poor practice; any irritation by the signaling hand will create a peevish reaction from the horse, a dislike of the exercise, and undesirable tense muscles.

As soon as the horse moves well to the lateral control (hand pressure and oral signal) on both sides, the lessons of the mounted turn on the forehand may begin.

To make this lesson more clear to the horse, this training should be begun with the horse's head to a wall or fence. Ride the horse straight at a wall and stop, remaining in rein contact. Obtain a slight left flexion, press down the left heel, move the left lower leg two or three inches to the rear and press the horse's barrel with the calf while giving the oral command, "Get over."

When the rider stops, he puts the horse "up to the bit," so to speak, and the fence makes it clear to the horse that the leg pressure calls for a lateral movement and is *not a forward leg control,* a point about which most horses are easily confused.

By depressing his heel the rider has shifted his weight to the left seat bone and has stretched his heel toward the ground. Now, when he applies calf pressure, his leg deep and firmly against the barrel, he must shift his weight toward, but not completely on, the right seat bone, *without bending at the waist.* This movement places the rider's balance in the direction of movement, and brings the controls (rein, leg, weight, and balance) together effectively.

If the horse refuses to step to the side with his rear legs, either the dismounted work was insufficient or the horse is willingly disobedient.

In the first case, more ground work is indicated. In the latter, flex the horse's neck to the left, as in dismounted work, until the haunches move one step to the right, then release all controls.

This rein effect is the *direct rein of opposition against the rear leg on the same side.* The rein acts directly upon the rear leg, causing it to yield and flex all of its joints.

It is absolutely necessary that the rider master the *direct rein of opposition* in all of its nuances, for obtaining "correct" bit obedience is almost impossible without it.

When the horse has learned the lateral control of the leg on both sides, he should be taken from the psychological crutch of the fence and have the turn on the forehand lessons repeated with the restraining control (cavesson) replacing the fence.

If he still attempts to move forward, defying the restraining control, increase the flexion until his haunches move laterally. Repeat this action until he answers the restraining control.

This rein action is a refinement of the disciplinary rein used when the horse was first led if he attempted to bolt. The trainer, unable to restrain the powerful forward force by holding straight back, stepped away to the side, allowing the lead rope to slip, braced himself and held. Running into the force at an angle, the horse bent himself around and stopped facing the trainer. The action would also come into play if the horse attempted to bolt straightaway on the lunge, or in driving reins.

When a horse defies the restraining control with an active resistance, he first clamps his lower jaw; then he stiffens his poll; the stiffness flows rapidly through his back to the rear legs that support all of the force against the bit or cavesson. In effect, he attempts to pull the trainer in much the same manner that he would pull a load with a harness, the difference being that he is pulling with his mouth or nose, instead of his shoulders.

As only the illusion that the trainer is more powerful than the horse enables us to control an animal with many times our strength, nothing should be allowed to shatter this illusion.

When the rider, unable to restrain the horse with a reasonable action on both reins, allows one rein to slip while holding hard on the other, he works against the horse's lateral weakness, and the horse finds that he must flex his stiff neck, his stiffened back, and finally, the root of the problem, the three stiffened joints of his rear legs. The direct rein of opposition (the force of which is relative to the resistance of the horse) has shown the horse that he must allow the restraining action to control (flex) his hind legs as they are forced to step to the side.

When the horse can be kept on the spot with an *easy* rein control, the turn of the forehand work may be continued.

13

Introduction of the Diagonal Leg

As soon as the horse has mastered the turn on the forehand, diagonal leg control may be introduced.

Up to now, we have been using *lateral* controls (leg and rein on the same side). We have been, while riding on the left rein (obtaining left flexion), allowing the lateral movement, initiated by our left leg, to dissipate by removing the left leg pressure and allowing the horse to gradually stop moving at will. Now we begin to apply right leg pressure and bring the lateral movement of the haunches to a halt with an active *diagonal* leg.

At first this leg will be relatively ineffective, but do not change the horse's flexion in order to use the direct rein of opposition, as you will then no longer be using a diagonal leg. Instead, urge the horse straight forward with both legs (forward control). Flopping the horse suddenly from one flexion to the other (a crude sawing action) is ruinous to the horse's mouth and neck muscles.

In a short time, the horse will respond to the stopping action of the diagonal leg. The turn on the forehand work should then be continued until the horse can do any number of steps to either side, half and full turns, and stop precisely on a desired leg.

Stopping the lateral
movement of a turn on
the forehand with the
diagonal leg

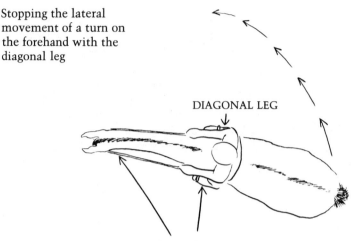

DIAGONAL LEG

LATERAL CONTROLS

PULSATING LEG

In movement like turn on the forehand the horse will move his haunches to the side by pushing against the ground with the leg on the side opposite the direction of movement.

Or, more simply stated, a horse flexed to the left will shove against the ground with his inside rear hoof (left) while raising his outside rear (right) leg in order to receive and support the displaced weight.

It is physically impossible for him to step to the right while his left hoof is raised; therefore, our active leg must not maintain an invariable (steady) pressure or we will be asking the horse to do the impossible—push himself sideways with the hoof that is in the air. Instead our leg must pulsate invisibly in time with the movement of the horse's inside, propelling leg (the leg on the side to which he is flexed). Otherwise we invite a loss of respect on the horse's part for the trainer's superior intelligence.

LEG YIELDING

As soon as our horse is doing obedient stationary turns on the forehand, we introduce the same movement at the walk.

To begin, we ride at a walk on a large circle (sixty-foot diameter) to our left, and with the inside rein we flex the horse's neck to an arc that describes the path he follows. Our previous stationary flexion work makes this possible. If the horse should refuse, by stiffening his neck, to flex his neck to a reasonable signal, repeat the neck flexion lesson while walking.

With the horse at a calm walk on the circle, neck slightly flexed to the inside, next depress your inside heel with a slight shift of the weight to the inside seat bone, and press with the leg moved to the rear two or three inches while simultaneously shifting the weight toward, but not completely on, the outside seat bone, giving the oral command, "Get over."

The controls are exactly the same as in the stationary turn on the forehand, but now, more than ever, the rider *must not stiffen*—he must remain supple and allow his hips to follow the motion of the walk. Were he to stiffen, the horse would automatically stiffen in resistance.

If the horse does not move his haunches one step to the outside, increase the flexion, using the neck as a lever, until the haunches yield to the side, then release all lateral controls and continue walking on the circle. When the horse has regained the calm walk, again attempt to "leg" his haunches to the outside.

Soon, the horse will yield to the inside leg and be able to walk a few steps with his forefeet on the original circle and his hind feet on a slightly larger circle (two tracks). When this point is reached, we will repeat the leg yielding exercise at the trot, where, due to the period of suspension, it will be easier for the horse.

We generally introduce new movements at the walk because of its slow, calming influence. As soon as the horse understands, we begin the work at the trot.

14

First Position

As a logical progression from leg yielding, we will now be able to teach our horse to assume what I call *first position* on a curved track.

First position and *second position* are the two exceptions to the rule that a horse's rear hooves must exactly follow his fore hooves while on one track. (*Second position* will be discussed later.) *First position* is a necessary exception because of the demand for lateral flexion of the horse's body when he is traveling on curved lines and, because as a horse becomes more collected, his rear legs must travel more closely together in order to be able to engage, not only more forward under the load, but more to the lateral center of the load.

The thrust of the rear legs must be in the direction of the forehand in order to act against it and produce relative lift of the forehand.

A horse who is supple and well trained and has good conformation will naturally assume the *first position* on curved lines.

If you will closely observe your horse at a relaxed trot on the lunge, you will notice that at times his inside rear hoof does not track the corresponding foreleg; it is placed one half a hoof width to the inside in order to get more directly under the weight shift caused by flexion and the centrifugal force of the circle. When this happens the horse has naturally assumed *first position.*

Although a horse may naturally choose the correct *first position* on a curved track, he may also choose *not* to assume it in order to evade: proper longitudinal flexion, carrying an even load on each rear leg, moving forward with sufficient impulsion, obedience to the rider's controls.

Various kinds of evasions and difficulties can be corrected with the proper application of first and second position. There are horses that travel very "heavy on the forehand," usually the result of a forced bowing of the neck, with excessively straddled rear legs. The thrust of the spread rear legs can never be directed toward relieving the load on the forehand. The thrust of each rear leg misses, so to speak, due to this misalignment. This type of horse can never be collected until its rear legs can be made to track more closely together.

There are horses that turn out one or both rear legs from the hip joint, as for example, a brood mare in the last days of gestation (pregnancy) is forced to do by her swollen abdomen. This type of horse can never be collected until the thrust of his turned-out rear legs is realigned and forced to work against the forehand.

By being able to *position* his horse, the trainer will be able to direct the thrust of the rear legs against the forehand so that it will be used efficiently.

To place our horse in *first position*, we enter an easy turn using only the leading rein and a slight shift of balance into the turn. If the horse is unconstrained, he will flex his neck and ribs to the curve of the turn, but if he attempts an evasion, he will not flex at the ribs, therefore his rear hooves will go off of the trace of the curve—he will have become crooked. To prevent this crookedness, the rider must assist the flexing rein with the inside leg. If, then, the horse flexes at the ribs, he will assume *first position*. If he continues to resist by remaining stiff to the leg, the rider must continue the leg and "back it up" by increasing the flexion with the rein. When the horse finally

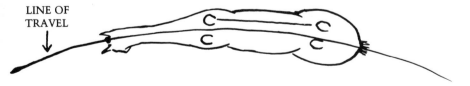

First position: The outside rear hoof tracks the outside fore hoof; the inside rear hoof steps inside the trace of the inside fore hoof by one-half a hoof's width.

yields to step sideways with his haunches, he will flex at the ribs, and his inside rear leg will track closer to the outer rear leg. By repeating this exercise each time the horse tries to follow a curved line with a stiff body, the rider "shows" the horse that he must flex at the ribs to the leading rein, backed up by the inside leg, if necessary, the rein and leg being used alternately, and soon the rider will be able to easily place the horse in *first position* with the inside rein and leg. He will be able, by asking the horse to yield to the inside leg, not enough to move laterally but only flexing in preparation to moving laterally, to move the inside rear leg closer to the outer rear leg by one half a hoof width.

15

Obedience to the Restraining Control

Now that our horse understands the lateral displacing action of the inside rein and leg, we can begin to teach him obedience to the restraining control.

A horse may refuse to obey the restraining control in a number of different ways. He may yield his head and neck to the rein action, bowing his neck instead of allowing the restraining rein to slow the action of his rear legs, in which case the horse's timing (the rhythm of the gait) stays the same, and the restraining rein becomes a neck-bending rein that merely moves the horse's mouth closer to his chest (false compliance to the bit).

When a horse is in this position it is referred to as *behind the bit.*

He may passively resist the rein action by raising his head and "eweing" his neck (stargazing), and again the rein becomes a neck-bending rein that does not affect the rear legs and cause a slowing of pace.

The "ewe-necked stargazer" must first be allowed to walk on a completely loose hanging rein until his head has dropped to a normal position (neck horizontal to the ground). The rider then tries for light rein contact and continues the walk. If the horse, through

Behind the bit

habitual fear of the bit, raises his head, the rider must return to the free rein until the head lowers, when he again seeks light contact. This work is time consuming and demands great patience and tact on the part of the trainer, but eventually the horse will regain its confidence in the rider's hands and accept light contact without raising his head.

All use of apparatus, tie-downs, etc., will fail in retraining the confirmed "stargazer," for they will only achieve a forced compliance, as they act directly on the horse's body, not on his mind. If the vice, obsession, or fixation is not corrected at the source, *the horse's mind*, then the horse has not been retrained, only mechanically restrained.

Active resistance to the restraining control is more commonly encountered. In this type of resistance, the horse clamps his lower jaw, stiffens his neck, back, and rear legs against the restraining control, and continues in the same timing, or sometimes increasing both timing and speed.

A second type of active resistance, which usually evolves when the first remains uncorrected, is when the horse actually attempts to pull the reins from the rider's hands. Many horses also learn this in self-defense against heavy-handed riders who continue to hold a heavy fixed-hand long after the horse has stopped or slowed (or try to nag a horse's head into a falsely bowed position).

All types of resistance to the restraining control must be corrected before further training can continue, for a horse in any state of resistance will be psychologically incapable of learning, and his action cannot be correct—his stride will be cramped and shortened.

As we have already introduced the direct rein of opposition to the horse in order to be able to hold him on the spot for a turn on the forehand, it will be relatively easy to use this rein to overcome resistance to the restraining control.

It is best to introduce the restraining control while practicing stops from the walk, and a short description of a correctly executed stop is needed to clarify our goal.

With the horse at a calm walk, in light contact with the hands, we increase the pressure of the contact, rock to the forward edge of our seat bones, our hips tilting forward more than our shoulders. (This movement serves two purposes: it relieves the load on the horse's loins and rear legs—the parts that will need freedom to stop correctly—and simultaneously signals the horse, through the shift of saddle pressure on his back, that a change is coming.) We now begin to slow the horse by gradually ceasing to follow the forward movement with our hands, withdrawal of the hands, and continue the slowing until the horse comes smoothly to a stop, *with abso-*

The stargazer

lutely no sudden or jerky movements, and no perceptible movement of the head or mouth to the rear. In other words, we signal the horse to obediently slow to a stop so smoothly that he does not stop in mid-stride, one leg far ahead of the other, but is able to bring his rear-most leg up and stand squarely.

One fault that frequently mars the performance of a correct stop is the sudden premature stopping of a lazy horse who is waiting and longing for any hint of a stop signal. The rider's legs must remain vigilant and prevent these sudden premature stops wherein the horse loses his forward impulsion and sags to a back-dropping stop. The horse must be made to continue the impulsion of the walk until he stops. At times, this lazy response fools the novice rider into believing that his horse has achieved perfect obedience, where in reality, the horse is not stopping obediently: he is quitting.

During the stops, the rider must try to use his hands exactly as in driving on the lunge without tightening his back. The back must remain relaxed, allowing the hips to follow the rhythmical motion of the horse. Only in this way will the hands remain elastic and not incite resistance in the horse.

If the horse, through contrariness or direct defiance, stiffens his neck against the restraining rein, the rider must anchor his seat bone on one side, brace his back, and hold hard on one rein, while allowing the other rein to slip, until the horse's rear legs take *one* step to the side. After one lateral step, the rider must allow the horse to straighten, resume his crotch-relief seat and again signal the horse to slow. If a second refusal is encountered, the rider must repeat the above action. This lateral displacement of the haunches must be repeated until the horse responds to a positive but light restraining signal by slowing to a stop without *stiffening his poll or neck.*

Only a horse that responds to the bit without stiffening is truly obedient to the bit. A horse that will reduce his forward speed in response to a painless, soft signal is under control and will gradually come to a stop.

Of course, these stops are not the sudden full halts of an advanced horse, for full halts are impossible with an uncollected horse, nor should they be attempted.

When an uncollected horse is stopped abruptly, he lowers or raises his head and stops on his forefeet, usually in a series of rough bounces, and the resultant extreme concussions in the joints of his forelegs bring on a premature arthritic condition.

Displacing haunches at a walk for discipline

There is one more method of correcting resistance to the restraining control in common use that deserves discussion if only to expose it to the public for the barbaric, unnecessary cruelty to horses that it is. It is the act of hitting the horse over the head with the hand, a crop, or in some cases, a piece of pipe.

The horse, the innocent victim, usually learns to raise his head to evade the pain of a rough hand or a curb bit that was fitted too soon. When this technique is used, when he raises his head in an attempt to evade the pain in his mouth, he is struck over the head. He must accept the pain in his mouth or have the pain compounded by a blow to the top of his head.

Most horses learn to evade this double pain by going behind the bit (*see photo on page 98*). The trainer is then satisfied, not realizing, in his ignorance, that he has destroyed the horse's stride.

The above is not to say that a sharp hand slap to the ear (not the head) is out of place with a spoiled rearing horse that is attempting to intimidate his rider. When this type of horse rears, most always in a refusal to go forward, the rider must vigorously drive him forward with spurs and whip while slapping the ears to make the horse duck forward. Few riders have the seat and ability to retrain a confirmed rearer.

When the resisting horse has gained confidence in the bit and the rider's hands, and has accepted light rein contact, then the rider may attempt to stop from the walk, but he must be extremely careful not to cause pain in the horse's mouth and destroy the little confidence he has gained.

16

Stabilizing the Timing of the Trot

Now that we have the means to demand obedience through the restraining control, we will return to work at the trot, continuing to stand in the stirrups until the horse develops the necessary strength to support the weight added by our posting with a complete absence of discomfort.

Our first concern will be to keep the horse *on the rail* and prevent him from reducing the size of the area he travels. We will use the leading rein to keep the horse from cutting in toward the center of the arena.

This problem is more often encountered with lazy horses who seem to believe that it is shorter, and easier, to trot at a given rate for ten minutes on a small circle than on a large one. When the rider allows his horse to decrease the circle, he is encouraging this false supposition. This is not to say that the horse should be pushed tightly into the corners of the arena. On the contrary, the corners should be rounded into large easy turns.

As soon as the horse has learned to stay on the rail, we turn our attention to rate (speed) and timing (rhythm of steps).

A well-made horse with an abundance of natural impulsion will trot boldly and freely around the arena. This type of horse must first be allowed to choose the rate and timing at which he is most com-

103

fortable. He must be allowed to trot forward vigorously, even if, at first, he is rushing a bit from high spirits. But if, after three or four circuits of the arena, he hasn't settled into a more relaxed trot, his apparent high spirits are due to mental excitement and he must be slowed.

On the other hand, a slightly lazy horse will, after a few turns about the arena, slow to an over-relaxed, foot-dragging trot. He must be accelerated.

The horse with the perfect disposition (if one exists) will immediately choose the correct rate and timing, but as we must work with the average imperfect horse, it is our job to make the nervous, excitable horse calm, and the lethargic horse energetic. This, in one sense, is the object of training.

Our immediate goal, in either case, is to confirm the steady timing of the trot on light rein contact. If the rhythm of the steps remains in *time*, as if the horse were trotting to music, then he has achieved timing. The timing may be too fast or too slow, but as long as the length of stride and rhythm of the steps remain constant, the horse has timing.

During this work, we allow the horse to choose, within certain boundaries, a trot at a given rate and timing. From that moment on, any attempt to speed up the timing will be met with a restraining rein.

If, on the other hand, the horse should attempt to slow his timing, he should be prevented from doing so with the forward control.

For the rider to be successful at this work, he must have an inborn, or acquired, highly developed sense of rhythm, for he must be able to prevent rhythm changes almost before they occur.

When it seems that the horse has learned to maintain a steady timing, be it too fast or too slow, the rider must let the reins slip, until they are hanging free and swinging and put the horse, in a manner of speaking, *on parole*. If the horse maintains his timing, the previous work has been successful. If he attempts to increase the timing, he must be checked with the reins, ridden on contact for a short time, and then the attempt at riding on a free rein tried again. This procedure must be repeated until the horse learns to remain at a steady timing on a free rein.

This work is necessary, because even the hint of a rein or a slightly loosened rein can psychologically hold a horse back, and the *test of obedience is possible only when the horse is allowed the freedom to disobey.*

17

Hands and Reins

At this point, a short discussion of the different types of *hands* and *reins* is necessary to give a more precise understanding to the reader.

The rein, when a single rein is used, enters the hand (with the thumb uppermost) under the little finger. It then passes through a hollow hand and is held between the first and second joint of the index finger and the thumb. If a crop is held, the rein may pass between the little and ring finger, freeing the little finger to hold the crop.

The upper arm hangs loosely from the shoulder; like a string with a weight attached, it will remain vertical and independent of the angle of inclination of the upper body.

The forearm will be raised from the elbow and form a continuation of the straight line of the rein from the horse's mouth. The inside of the forearm will lightly touch the rider's side, and the wrists will be straight, with the back of the hand held on the same plane as the outside of the forearm.

The height of the horse's head will determine exactly where the rider will hold his hands, but in general they will be located relatively over the horse's withers, depending on the relation between the length of the rider's arms and the size of the horse.

The fitting rein, a rein that exactly fits the distance between the hand and the horse's mouth, will be adjusted by allowing the reins to slip (they are held so that they will slip should the horse trip and

Correctly held single rein

Forearm and rein in a straight line

suddenly need more head freedom for balance); or for a sudden temporary yielding hand, they may be advanced by opening and advancing the elbow. If a major adjustment is needed to shorten the rein, they are pulled through the rein hand with the opposite hand.

Minor adjustments to accommodate the horse's movement will first be made by fingers, and, second, by a *slight* withdrawal of the hand through movement of the relaxed shoulder and elbow joint.

There are innumerable different ways of using the reins. At this point, we will be mainly concerned with the three basic ones: contact, loosened rein, and a loose rein.

Riding on contact refers to having a contact felt by both the horse's mouth and the rider's hand. It is also known as a *following hand* in that the hand follows the natural movement of the horse's head. A hand that does not follow—a fixed hand—restricts the natural head movement and thus the horse's balance and stride. At the walk, the head bobs up and down and swings from side to side. The development of a free-swinging walk is impossible if the head motion is restricted. At the trot, the horse's head remains stationary in relation to his body, hence the hands may remain stationary. At the gallop, the horse's head bobs up and down again and needs to be followed.

A restraining rein is initially applied by fixing the upper arm and closing the hand. If more restraint is necessary, the wrists are turned inward. If still more restraint is needed, the hands are withdrawn.

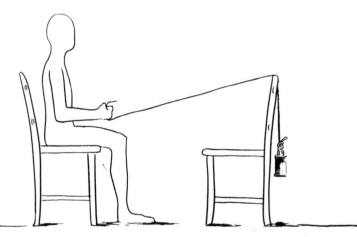

Rein/hand exercise: Lift the weight by opening and closing the hand

An excellent exercise for practicing contact with a horse's mouth and control is to hang a rein, with a small weight attached, over the back of a chair with the weight resting on the floor. Sit facing the chair, rein held properly, and practice raising and lowering the weight by opening and closing the hand.

A *loosened rein*, is effected by either advancing the hands or allowing the reins to slip until contact is lost; the rein is slightly slack, but contact may be quickly regained if necessary. This type of rein may have the effect of psychologically restraining the horse and prevent him from moving in complete freedom.

The *loose* or *free rein* is a rein loosened until it hangs down and swings freely under the horse's neck. The horse, seeing the reins swinging, knows that he has complete freedom and will be more apt to relax and regain a natural gait and stretch his neck muscles—or he may disobey and change his timing, rate, or direction.

A good seat is a prerequisite for a good hand. Unless the rider sits softly erect, in complete dynamic balance (in balance with the forward motion) with a strong confident seat, a good elastic, truly *independent hand* is impossible. An independent hand is one that is not affected by the movement of the body; i.e., it moves as if detached, floating, with a life and purpose of its own.

Many of my past students, students who thought they had achieved a perfectly independent hand, have been rudely disillusioned when I placed a glass of water in each of their hands, with the rein, and had them ride at the walk, trot, and gallop about the arena, their wet clothes attesting to their degree of inability. Of course, this test may only be passed, in all gaits, on an advanced horse that moves on elastically engaged haunches.

18
Regulated Timing

Once the horse has learned to maintain a steady rhythm at the trot the rider may begin to slightly adjust the timing.

If the horse is rushing or hurrying his timing must be slowed until he is swinging along freely with no unnecessary expenditure of energy. He must be using only enough energy to maintain the timing and balance of himself and the rider. If his is too slow and he is overly relaxed, moving lethargically with dragging rear legs, the timing must be increased.

In this work, rate is relatively unimportant; it is *how* the horse trots, not *how fast.*

When the horse's muscles pulsate (flex and relax) rhythmically, when his energy output is low, and he demonstrates a steady, *regulated* timing on a loose rein, he will have reached the *unconstrained trot.*

The more time is spent in consolidating this gait in the horse, the better the finished horse will be. The unconstrained trot will be the basis for all further training.

Once the horse discovers the more comfortable, pleasant way of moving at the unconstrained trot, the more easily will he adopt it.

In all training periods, the horse will first be ridden calmly until he warms up and relaxes into the unconstrained trot before further work is attempted.

In all further work, the horse will be returned to an unconstrained gait whenever overexcitement (from applied discipline, shying, etc.) and tense, shortened movements occur.

It is much easier to describe an unconstrained trot than it is to achieve it.

The horse must be unconstrained mentally as well as physically.

The nervous, fearful horse, one that throws up his head and tightens his back muscles at each bird (or imaginary bird) that flits by, is the most difficult to put into an unconstrained state. On the other side of the coin, the lazy, contrary horse that hates to obey is nearly as difficult, as he tightens his muscles convulsively in order to hold back defiantly at each command.

It is well for the novice to realize that there are horses that *are not worth training*, before he breaks his heart trying to make something out of the impossible ones.

This is not to say that a horse is not worth training because at times he is difficult, for at least fifty percent of the difficulty lies in the rider. The old saying, "The fault of all horses sits in the saddle" becomes more true as we advance and discover our weaknesses.

No matter what problems a horse is born with, bad disposition, or conformation, or both, it is up to the rider to guide and mold him to the maximum of his potential—for, after all, we are the superior being.

And each horse, no matter what type, when the end of the long hard road of training is reached, will have taught the trainer many things, and he will be able to say, "I'm doing well with this horse because of what I learned from the last one."

Let us return to the difficulties encountered while striving for a high degree of unconstraint at the trot.

A horse uses his legs for three purposes: support, locomotion, and movement. While stationary, he obviously is using them for support alone. In any state of forward motion, he is using his legs for support, locomotion, and movement simultaneously. In the piaffe (a trot in place), he will use his legs for leg movement and support. While swimming, he will use his legs for locomotion and motion.

When at any gait the horse achieves the correct proportions of support, locomotion, and leg movement, he will develop dynamic equilibrium and become balanced, and through continued balanced work, he will develop natural poise.

The horse that continually rushes, after he has grown accustomed to carrying a rider, usually rushes from a refusal to use his legs as support. He is like a man falling forward whose feet are hurrying to catch up. His balance point lies ahead of the base of support formed by his four feet. He usually goes faster and faster at the trot until he falls into a loose gallop. He is rushing to evade the necessary, more difficult work of using his legs for support. Thus, he is rushing from laziness.

When this type of horse is trained to maintain a steady regulated timing, *on a loose rein*, he will find and develop his natural balance and gradually develop poise.

If the rider were naive (or foolish) enough to allow the horse the physical or psychological support in the rein at this point, the horse would be quick to capitalize on this weakness and turn the reins into a "head sling." He would balance on the rein *and not on his own four feet*.

As this type of horse must be frequently checked in his attempts to rush when given a *loose rein*, it will make the rider's task easier if he holds both reins in the left hand. In this manner, he can quickly adjust the slack with his right hand.

Riding with reins in one hand

The lazy horse that moves as if his feet were glued to the ground uses his legs for support, but uses mostly the bones and locked joints, not his muscles, and rapidly becomes loose jointed, his original potential for an expressive fluid stride permanently lost.

The lazy horse must be brought to life by continually accelerating him to an unconstrained trot where his muscles equally flex and relax.

Do not make the mistake of using a constant forward control to achieve this acceleration. Any control applied too hard or for too long a time will accustom the horse to ignoring the control and achieve the exact opposite result of that desired by the rider.

Instead, when the horse's trot begins to drag, urge him forward until the proper timing is regained, then relax the forward control and remain vigilant for the first sign of faltering. The horse must learn to trot at the proper rhythm with the rider completely passive, merely going along.

However, as with all commands, the forward command must be applied until the horse responds.

This is one of the most often violated rules of horsemanship. The aid is usually misapplied as follows: A mounted rider applies the forward control by a forward shift of weight and leg pressure. The horse balks and refuses to move forward. The rider increases the leg pressure. Still the horse refuses. Preparing to use the whip, *the rider relaxes the forward control for a moment and then reapplies it*, followed by a blow from the crop, and the horse shoots forward.

During the few seconds that the rider ceased the forward control, the horse won the battle: *he did not obey the original command*, although he was forced to obey the second command. He now knows that he can successfully disobey a command.

Another example of this, frequently seen in a schooling arena is a rider on a "sticky" horse, one that suddenly refuses a left turn and runs to the gate. Most young novices, because the horse is resisting the left rein so strongly, switch to the right rein and pull the horse around. Again, the horse has won the battle of the wills—he successfully disobeyed the command, in this case that of following the leading left rein.

When a rider gives a command, meets resistance, and yields, for whatever reason, the horse will think that the rider yielded because of weakness, fear, or ignorance, and he will be encouraged to disobey again. In other words, his training is going *backwards*.

A professional trainer is very careful about which commands he gives to a horse, for he knows that he must follow through, without exception, or lose dominance over the horse.

A good rule is: Do not give commands, either on the ground or mounted, unless you feel you are able to enforce them. There is a definite responsibility to giving commands—the responsibility of backing them up.

Many times a command will result in a direct battle of wills, and call for a showdown. If the rider yields—backs down—he is through with that horse, at least until he gains the courage and ability to face the challenge—and win!

This is what I call the "Wounded Tiger Syndrome." I have read that, in India, each section has its "tiger hunter" to eliminate the man killers that periodically appear. The tiger hunter is a highly respected man and has great social status. If he wounds a tiger, it is the unwritten code that he go into the jungle, where the angry tiger waits, and finish him off. If he refuses, and another must do his dirty work, he is finished as a hunter, and his social position will be reduced to that of an untouchable. The moral is: *Finish off your own wounded tigers, or don't pull the trigger.*

Many times, as an instructor, I have been forced into the position of finishing someone else's "wounded tiger" due to the inability of the student. This is quite acceptable and a normal part of an instructor's job, for there are riders who unknowingly create "wounded tigers" and are excused because of ignorance. The riders who are inexcusable are the the ones who knowingly, by hiding their fear, create a hidden wounded tiger for their instructor, one for which he is totally unprepared.

If you are being slightly intimidated or are compromising your commands in a subtle unseen way; if you are accepting conditional surrender from your horse, and slowly, in a covert way, lighting the fuse to a future explosion of a showdown, be honest with your instructor—tell him you are spoiling the horse and give him a fighting chance. Don't send him into the dark jungle ignorant of the wounded tiger that waits in the shadows. And don't create and feed a tiger that you will have to kill one day; kill the ugly cub of insubordination when it is first born, before it becomes too big for you.

19

Riding Out of the Arena

When the horse is settled in the unconstrained trot, when he has developed natural balance and a degree of poise, we will begin to ride him out of the arena.

It is impossible to correctly train a horse by riding only in an arena. The horse regards the arena as a schoolboy regards school: he likes it, but enough is enough.

He needs long quiet walks, interspersed with some trotting on inviting straight stretches, in order to refresh his mind and develop self-reliance. He should be given a loose rein so that he can look about and use his head and neck freely to develop his natural balance on the changing slopes.

On his first few ventures out of the arena, he should be accompanied by an older, well-trained horse, one ridden by an understanding and considerate rider. The older horse should be ridden to the left and slightly ahead of the young horse so as to lend moral support.

While passing fear-inspiring objects, terrible little white dogs, or horse-eating cows, allow the older horse to go first, forming a sort of moving barrier between the frightened horse and the fearful object.

After a few days, you will be able to take the young horse over the same trails alone. If he becomes shy of any object, *do not at-*

tempt to ride him up to it; detour around it while maintaining the forward pace.

Any attempt to ride the horse up to a fearful object to "show him it won't hurt him" will create immediate terror in the horse and he will refuse. The rider will then be forced to use his whip, and when the horse, totally concentrating on the object that may be dangerous, suddenly feels pain, it becomes entrenched in his mind that the fearful object is definitely dangerous!

On the other hand, a horse of a different character may be quick to capitalize on the in-depth inspection of all suspicious objects and spend the entire trail ride stopping and sniffing.

The best technique is to pass by quickly, detouring if necessary, the rider remaining calm, as if the fearful object did not exist.

20

Adding the Bit Rein

As his training progresses, the horse, having discovered that the unconstrained gaits are more comfortable, gained strength from the daily workouts, and regained his natural balance with the added weight of the rider, will enter into an unconstrained state more quickly, and the lungeing period, with which each training period should begin, may be shortened proportionately.

Up to this point, we have been riding with the reins attached to the side-rings of the cavesson, with the bit attached to the cavesson in such a way that a little of our rein action has been transferred to the bit and felt by the horse's mouth.

In this manner, the horse has slowly become accustomed to responding to signals on the bridge of his nose and, to a lesser degree, signals to his mouth.

As the horse progresses, and strong rein action rarely becomes necessary, we will wish to transfer our rein signals to the more sensitive mouth in order to refine our rider-horse communication and our control.

For a short transition period, we will add another small bit-attachment strap from the bit to the noseband of the cavesson and another pair of reins to the bit. The bit-attachment straps will run from the bit rings forward to the noseband and will transfer the rein action to the noseband, thus making heavy action on the bit impossible.

Cavesson rein pressure moves the bit

Additional strap for transference of bit pressure to noseband

During this period, we will ride almost entirely with the cavesson rein, only gradually using the bit.

The double reins will be held with the cavesson rein entering the hand over the index finger, and the bit rein entering under the little finger. The reins will pass each other and be held between the thumb and index finger.

With the reins held in this manner, we can, by opening our fingers, use the cavesson rein independently, or, by closing our fingers, use the bit rein independently. All degrees of rein pressures are possible: Using both reins equally, seventy-five percent cavesson and twenty-five percent bit rein, etc.

We begin by riding exactly as we did before we added the bit rein, completely on the cavesson. Then, very gradually, we loosen the noseband, and use more and more bit. We continue in this manner, transferring the pressure and signals from the cavesson to the bit, as long as the horse does not demonstrate mouth discomfort. If the horse develops symptoms of an "unhappy mouth" such as excessive gaping, raising the tongue in an attempt to get it over the bit, sticking his tongue out the side of his mouth, gnashing the bit angrily, or stiffening and traveling unnaturally in any way, we will ride with the bit rein slacked, entirely on the cavesson rein.

This transitory period is critical. Many horses have been ruined by impatient, tactless riders during the transition from cavesson to bit.

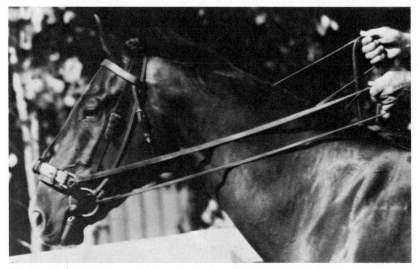

Position of cavesson and bit reins in hands

21

Acceleration

The horse, when his unconstrained trot can be easily regulated with no force of hand or leg, is ready for acceleration.

We begin with a horse swinging along, his timing as steady as a metronome, at an unconstrained posting trot on a loose rein. We pick up the reins and make light positive contact. The horse must continue his pace completely unchanged. If he raises his head, opens his mouth, slows, stiffens, or gives any signs of discomfort or fear of the rider's hands, the mental and physical lack of constraint has been lost and further progress is impossible for the moment.

A horse that is well trained at this point will make absolutely no visible change when the rein is changed from loose to contact, or vice versa. There will be an invisible mental change; the horse will have been prepared for a change and thus be attentive.

If the horse correctly accepts the rein contact we then apply the forward control, along with the verbal command "Come on." Our leg should pulsate in rhythm with the trot and our posting, when we ask the horse to accelerate.

What we wish to happen is that the horse obediently thrust forward with his rear legs, increasing the length of his stride while maintaining the same timing and unconstraint. Alas, this is when most riders "drop the ball." The horse merely increases his rhythm, *not his stride*, or tightens in resentment, or fear, or disobedience to the forward control.

Loading seat on a collected horse: the piaffe

I continually try to impress my students with the fact that most horses do not become "good" because they are just not obedient enough.

Riders tend to become satisfied too easily, thinking that their horse has reached the pinnacle of perfect obedience, and as most of them have never seen a truly obedient horse, it is understandable why they fall into this trap.

There are certain psychological states necessary before a horse will accelerate correctly.

The first is mental unconstraint. The horse must have accepted the weight of the rider and be comfortable with the rider's seat. If the rider's seat becomes hard (a stiff tense rider), the jar and the lack of elastic harmony with the rhythm of the horse's movements will irritate the horse, and mental unconstraint will be lost.

One cause of this is the rider abandoning the crotch-relief seat and sitting erect or backward, thus loading the back and rear legs that are not ready. The resulting pain will cause the horse to lose mental unconstraint and the symptoms of physical constraint will appear (hollow back and dragging rear legs). This seat, the rider sitting erect, or slightly behind vertical, with his pelvis tilted back and his back braced, is used for fully collecting an advanced, supple horse, but it is usually used on a horse that is past the opposite

Loading seat on a collected horse: the canter

Loading seat on an uncollected horse

extreme of a collected horse; that is, one who is hollow-backed and stargazing or falsely collected. *The seat must conform to the degree of collection achieved by the horse.*

If the seat is faulty, the hands will be faulty. Soft elastic hands cannot exist without a good seat. Poor hands create pain in the horse's mouth, and mental constraint will always be the result of pain.

But let us say that the seat and hands are good, as evidenced by the unconstrained mental state of the horse, but still the horse loses his unconstraint upon being asked to accelerate.

The problem then becomes one of cooperation—the horse does not want to obey. Yet the horse *must* want to obey, for any use of force, or threat of force, will destroy the mental unconstraint; and the horse will respond incorrectly with a shortened, choppy stride.

Now we are getting to the nucleus of horsemanship: *how to get a horse to want to obey.* When the horse's will is completely subordinated to the will of the rider, he will come to believe that he must obey, that any resistance is futile, and, therefore, he will form the habit of wanting to obey. Through consistent, direct, association of ideas—disobedience and discomfort versus obedience and comfort—he will come to choose, actually seek, obedience, but only if he considers the rider a superior being, more intelligent, stronger, but also a friend who loves him.

A horseman with "feel" will intuitively find hundreds of ways to convince the horse of his superiority.

One way is not allowing the horse to rub his head on him. He realizes that to allow the horse this liberty would cause the horse to regard him as an equal, but that to strike the horse in the head would sever friendly relations as well as produce a head-shy horse. So, while rubbing his horse behind the ear, if the horse attempts to rub his hand, he commences to pat the horse, speaking softly all the while, but patting with enough force to cause discomfort. The horse realizes that the "caress" is uncomfortable and ceases to lean his head into the strong patting, whereupon the person returns to rubbing the horse's head.

The person has controlled the situation without resorting to anger or direct use of force, thus reestablishing his superiority.

Another way in which riders unknowingly destroy a horse's unconstraint and his desire to obey is by the application of irritating or painful signals.

If the pressure signals (leg, bit, etc.) produce an uncomfortable sensation in the horse, he will anticipate the discomfort and become "flinchy." He will greet each signal with a tense reaction, sort of bracing for the rough signal; or worse, he will flick his ears back in an effort to threaten the rider.

The signals must be painless, pain only applied when direct disobedience is encountered. Until the rider learns to feather his pressure signals, apply them with a velvet touch, but with a positive pressure that the horse can easily feel, he will continue to fail to produce a well-trained horse.

Of course, there is, and perhaps will always be, the spoiled horse who will also accelerate improperly.

The completely spoiled horse offers no real problem, for one soon comes to a showdown with him and completely dominates him, or one fails and acquires a different horse.

The partially spoiled horse is the one that poses the most difficulty for the novice. This is the horse that obeys sluggishly, in his own sweet time, but with the sour expression that clearly tells the rider, "I'll do a little of what you ask, but don't push me or I'll throw you on your head!"

The horse is obeying, in a sense, but he is "talking back" disrespectfully. The novice rider is usually reluctant to discipline this type of horse, and when told to do so usually responds with, "But he did what I told him to do!" A horse must never be allowed to successfully threaten the rider. He must obey with no "back talk," for mental resistance is a far cry from mental unconstraint.

At each threatening gesture to the forward control, he must be struck smartly on the side behind the rider's leg with the crop. To do otherwise would convince the horse that the rider is either ignorant or afraid, and neither trait will demonstrate the rider's superiority.

When the horse's mind is in a comfortably obedient state, as evidenced by his obedience to regulating signals and an unconstrained trot, he will accelerate properly by shoving off strongly with his rear legs.

The rider will feel the powerful thrust, and the horse's rate will increase as the strides grow longer, while the timing remains constant.

The visible evidence that the action of the haunches is correct is in front of the rider: the horse's nose will first go forward and then down. The rider's hands must advance and allow the horse to stretch forward, and reach for the bit.

After a few strides of acceleration, we relax our forward control and allow the horse to return to the ordinary unconstrained trot. We are not interested in having our horse travel indefinitely at an extended trot; we are interested only in the acceleration itself, and the physical effect it has produced in the horse.

When the horse truly accelerates, when he wants to go forward and allows the rider to drive him forward, the *automatic response* of correctly activated rear legs stretches the entire spine and lowers the horse's head.

When the head is advanced forward and down, the neck (cervical) muscles, which are attached to the thoracic vertebrae (withers), pull these forward. The withers, attached by muscles to the vertebrae behind them, in turn raise the back, a back that was sagging and could not pulsate properly.

The rear legs, thrusting vigorously through the action of the powerful haunch muscles, have tipped the rear of the pelvis (ischium) closer to the ground, thus the muscles attaching the pelvis to the back are stretched, raising the back from the rear. This phenomenon of raising the back by lowering the head may be seen by pushing a gentle horse's head down while he is standing relaxed; the back behind the withers will be seen to rise.

Of course, any attempt to force a horse's head down while riding will fail to restore proper action; the force will cause the horse to travel more heavily on the forehand because the lifting effect of the thrusting rear legs is missing.

The driving rear legs lift the load from the forehand in much the same manner as a bicycle or motorcyle lifts the front wheel while doing a "wheelie."

Thus when the horse's action is correct the vertebrae of the back will be stretched, like a string of beads or a bridge truss, and returned to the arched position that is natural. When the back is tense or hollow it cannot act as a shock absorber for the fore and rear legs.

22

Stretching in Hand and Slowing

The act of accelerating a horse while at an unconstrained trot is called "stretching the horse in hand." It is a movement natural to all horses and may be seen in young horses at play in the pasture, when they race forward, if they truly want to go forward. It may also be seen at the horse races in the stretch. When horses race for the wire, they will be stretched—if they truly want to win.

In this essential movement, this stretching the horse in hand, many riders fail and produce a hurried run, creating a horse that has his center of balance ahead of his feet and is, in a manner of speaking, *running off his feet.*

The key to the rider's failure to stretch the horse in hand lies in his failure to understand what is meant by *in hand.* In hand means that the horse is under control, *especially the control of the hands!*

Often, after a few extensions on the long side of the arena (the acceleration must be on straight lines) a spirited horse will begin to anticipate the acceleration with gusto, and at the signal will fly forward completely out of control, running away at the trot. He will then be *out of hand!*

The horse must remain obedient to the bit before, during, and after acceleration. In fact, the test of every rider lies in his ability to keep the horse obedient to the bit during every movement that he executes.

Once contact through the reins is obtained, the horse must be made to obey all of the signals it receives through these lines of communication. To do otherwise would be untraining the horse.

This is not to say that a horse must always be ridden in hand. He should frequently be given a loose rein and left to his own devices—to follow a trail; jump a fence; negotiate broken ground; to rest his neck and back muscles—as long as he stays at the same rate and timing as when he was given the loose rein.

When the horse is responding nicely to the bit, by doing easy trot-walk transitions, he is ready for another attempt at stretching in hand.

Stretching in hand is done as follows: At an unconstrained trot, the reins are picked up and contact established. The rider *scarcely* begins to slow for a trot-walk transition *only enough to test the horse's willing compliance to the bit.* When this compliance is almost imperceptibly evident, the rider applies the accelerating command, keeping the horse *in hand,* but allowing him to stretch.

This stretching in hand, so easily accomplished on an advanced, well-trained horse, is not at all easy to teach to a young horse. It is also extremely difficult to execute in the retraining of the spoiled old horse that has learned to brace his deceitfully tightened back as a defense against any honest work.

After the horse has accelerated, stretching forward and increasing his stride, the rider must cease the forward control and gently slow to the original unconstrained trot.

It is important that the restraining signal be started before the horse ceases to increase his stride, while he is still accelerating.

The following is the effect we are trying to achieve in the horse: At the moment of receiving the signal to accelerate, the horse will push himself forward vigorously with the rear hoof that is grounded. The other rear leg will reach further forward in an unconscious effort to maintain equilibrium. After grounding, this leg will shove off strongly as it comes behind vertical, and the process will repeat itself. The strides will have become longer and the rear hooves will be grounded farther forward under the horse; the rear legs will be *engaged.* This engagement will continue until the horse reaches a faster rate where he will level off and return to a shorter stride at a faster timing.

The slowing rein effect must be begun before the acceleration ceases in order to cause the horse to slow on his *engaged* rear legs.

Slowing the trot with engaged haunches

If the correct moment is missed, the horse will slow from a shortened stride and throw his weight onto his forelegs.

By the simple act of accelerating correctly, we have engaged the rear legs farther forward, partially relieving the load on the forehand, and we have caused the horse to place more of a load on them while slowing. We are getting one foot through the door that leads to collection.

When the horse accelerates, engaging his rear legs, and slows *obediently,* he will begin to *bridle;* that is, he will flex at the poll while slowing—if he stays obedient to the bit, in hand; if the slowing is done gently; if he does not stiffen from hard hands.

The rider must be careful not to slow to more than the original rate.

The complete sequence is: From the unconstrained trot we accelerate, cease our forward signal, receive the impulsion we have created in our hands, and slow to the original trot.

This work must be continued until it becomes easy and comfortable.

If this work seems unduly difficult and time consuming, the rider must remind himself that collection is impossible in the horse that cannot be stretched in hand!

23

Work with Cavaletti

The use of cavaletti, at this time, will aid the horse to stretch forward as well as his ability to negotiate broken ground, his general handiness and balance.

The cavaletti must be six to eight inches high and five to seven feet in length. They must be immovable—cavaletti that move when struck by the horse will be more harmful than beneficial.

The horse must be first taken over one cavaletti rail at a walk, on a completely free rein, until he can pass over it exactly in the center at a ninety degree angle, with no change of timing.

When he can correctly walk over one cavaletti, another may be added at a distance that will be determined by the horse's stride. He must be able to take a normal step at a steady rhythm and not be forced to take a short half-step.

As his ability progresses, more cavaletti may be added, until he can easily walk over four or five. The distance between the cavaletti will be four or five feet. They must be moved closer if the horse takes extra steps.

It is imperative that the horse learn, by himself, on a loose rein how to step over, *not jump* the cavaletti with the rider sitting lightly at the walk or posting a vigorous trot. When we begin to trot over the cavaletti, we will start again with one and gradually increase to four or five.

Cavaletti work at the trot

If the cavaletti are too wide, the horse cannot be compelled to follow a straight line over their centers; if they are too high, so as to cause the horse to stumble or jump, the horse will be forced to tighten his back, and the opposite of a suppling effect will be achieved.

As the horse approaches the cavaletti, he will lower his head in order to see the obstacle more closely and determine his foot position so as to overcome it without stumbling. He will develop the ability to negotiate broken ground by learning to regulate his steps, and additionally, this lowering of the head, stretching forward, will encourage him to do so while moving at speed.

The principal gait for this work will be a vigorous trot. Cavaletti work at the gallop, when the horse must jump each obstacle, will be delayed until the horse is more advanced and ready to begin his jumping training.

24

On the Bit

When the horse can easily stretch in hand it is time to teach him to go on the bit. This is done by using the forward control to ask for the stretch in hand, but this time, after the horse has stretched a little, his head lowering and his nose advancing, we will not advance our hands to follow further head movement. Instead, we will drive the horse into our hands, sustaining the forward impulsion; the horse will come onto the bit and become supple.

It is the rider's forward control that puts the horse *on the bit*, with the hands passively accepting, never actively trying to pull in the horse's head. The rider must feel that the horse, in attempting to stretch further, came into his hands as a result of his response to the forward control.

There are riders who have misunderstood the term "on the bit," and have taught the horse, through constantly "nagging" with the hands, tight side-reins, or tie-down apparatuses, to falsely comply to the bit by bending the neck at the poll, or, as is more commonly seen, at the third cervical vertebra.

These horses, upon receiving a bit signal, merely bend the poll and continue on, ignoring the signal to slow their rate, and so the *slowing signal* becomes a *poll-bending* signal that puts the horse *behind the bit, not on the bit*. In fact, the horse will soon learn to overbend his neck to evade rein control!

A horse that is *behind the bit* is always *behind the leg,* and vice versa, and *behind the leg* means that a horse will not respond to the forward control.

130

When a horse is forced to bend his neck through active use of the hands, he bends his neck and tucks his nose closer to his chest. While doing so, he places more weight on his already overloaded forelegs, the very legs from which we are trying to lighten the load.

Putting the horse *on the bit*, a precursor to collection, is an attempt, through the vigorous thrusting of the rear legs partially sustained by the hands, to bring the support of the rear legs up under the horse and relieve the weight on the forehand. This cannot be done only with the action of the hands on the horse's mouth.

The stretching of a horse's neck when he goes on the bit is only an indicator that the action of the rear legs is correct. To believe that making the horse assume a certain position of the head and neck can cause the action of the rear legs to be correct is most erroneous.

The rider will be successful in putting the horse on the bit only when he realizes that the horse must increase the contact by attempting to stretch forward. In other words, the horse places more pressure on the bit with complete confidence in the rider's hands, a pressure that he chooses, a pressure with which he can be comfortable. The horse takes the contact on the rider's hands, not the hands on the horse!

Falsely on the bit—pulled from behind

On the bit

When the horse comes on the bit and becomes supple, he will begin to softly chew, not gnash, the bit; this is a sure sign that suppleness has been achieved.

Once the horse is on the bit, the rider's passive legs must become vigilant and allow no loss of impulsion. He must reapply the forward control if the horse attempts to cease his vigorous action and fall heavily on the bit or raise his head over the bit.

The temptation to move the hands backward to maintain the contact must be resisted; the horse must be continually stretched forward into the sustaining hands.

In beginning on-the-bit work, do not keep the horse on the bit for more than a short period, as he will tire rapidly and attempt to fall heavily on the forehand and on the bit in order to relieve his tired rear legs.

A relaxation of the hands and the forward urging position will allow the horse to return to the unconstrained trot.

The effect we have achieved by placing the horse on the bit is as follows: We caused a vigorous engagement of the rear legs by accelerating the horse. While the rear legs were thrusting forward, well engaged, we asked for more acceleration and received this added action in our hands. Where previously we ceased our forward control upon using the restraining control, we now continue to urge the

Falsely on the bit

horse forward while restraining him and the horse will come on to the bit. His engaged rear legs will flex as they did previously in slowing, but they will do so now without slowing the timing or rate or losing the action gained by acceleration. When the horse becomes supple, when he comes on to the bit, flexing his poll, he will have achieved the beginning of equestrian carriage, an acquired carriage, a carriage gained only through correct systematic exercises.

You might think of putting a horse on the bit in these terms: A horse is trotting at ten miles per hour. He is accelerated to fifteen miles per hour, but the hands allow him to reach only fourteen miles per hour, although he must continue to strive for fifteen miles per hour. Striving to reach the last mile puts him on the bit—where he must stay without forward leg pressure.

After a few weeks of consistent work, it will become easy to place the horse on the bit—but there are pitfalls to be avoided.

Some intelligent horses, usually of a lazy character, move their heads down and back, putting a heavy, dead pressure on the rider's hands. These horses are not on the bit but are merely going through the motions that have enabled them to evade honest work and satisfy the demands of an ignorant rider. These horses are actually lugging on the bit, balancing on the rider's hands, instead of actively engaging their haunches and balancing on their own four legs.

The horse that goes *falsely* on the bit in this manner is no longer in hand. He will no longer answer the bit.

The other general type of horse likely to evade going properly on the bit is the spirited horse with an overabundance of natural impulsion. He readily accelerates, stretching in hand, reaching for the bit, but when he reaches the bit, he attempts to *go right on through it. He bores on the bit.* He continues to accelerate until his trot goes out of time. He loses his unconstraint. He is no longer in hand. He is actually running away. The rider feels the mouth become hard and is suddenly surprised that he can no longer restrain the charging horse.

At the instant that the rider feels the mouth go hard (the neck and poll will stiffen), he must bring the horse to a complete stop, using disciplinary bit action if necessary.

Allowing a horse to charge around the arena in the apparent shape of being on the bit, even though the rate and timing may be constant, is detrimental, even fatal, to further training. The horse must remain in hand. The rider must be able to slightly regulate the rate and timing. In other words, the horse must be manageable. We are not attempting to create a more aesthetic appearance with the horse at the cost of control.

25

Full Halts and Half Halts

From the beginning, we had only our voice and our hands, through the cavesson, to stop the horse. These two controls and the horse's low level of training made it impossible to effect a beneficial sudden halt, so we prudently slowed the horse gradually to a stop.

We continued to use this manner of restraint until the horse became familiar with the holding action of the cavesson; then we were able to demand a higher degree of obedience to the voice and cavesson, while mounted, at the walk and with a stationary horse— we were able to begin bit obedience training.

In conjunction with bit obedience training, the horse learned to respond to the inside rein and leg. He also learned the irresistible force of the *direct rein of opposition,* the inside rein that can laterally displace his haunches and force his rear legs to flex when they stiffen in resistance to the bit.

Now that the horse is capable of coming onto the bit, has learned to respond to the combined action of the back, legs, weight, and reins, and has developed the necessary strength in the haunches, we can ask for full halts at the trot, but only as a disciplinary action to counteract boring, or leaning, on the bit. The time is not yet ripe for practicing full halts as an exercise. The horse will be ready for soft, collected full halts when he can easily maintain the collected trot.

A disciplinary full halt is applied in the following manner: With the horse at a working trot, on the bit, the rider attempts to slow slightly and discovers that the mouth has gone dead. The horse does not respond; he is not on the bit, but boring on it. To continue would teach the horse to trot stiffly, out of control. The rider must stop and regain control. If he merely pulls on the reins, he will force the horse's head behind or over the bit and teach the horse other methods of evading it.

The rider must follow the rule "legs before reins," advance his hands lightly and apply the forward control. As soon as the horse responds by increasing his rate of engagement of the rear legs and hindquarters, the rider restrains with the bit, continuing the forward control, forcing the horse more on the bit and making him stop on his engaged rear legs. He must keep the horse pushed up to the bit with the forward control while coming to a stop in a series of shortened steps. The restraining hands are limited by the relative effectiveness of the forward control to keep the horse on the bit. If they exceed it, they will put the horse over or behind the bit, allowing the disobedient, stiffened rear legs to successfully evade the bit.

This method of disciplinary full halt will be sufficient for most horses, but there are horses who, upon receiving the forward control, wildly or stubbornly clamp their jaws, stiffen their necks and backs, and continue to bore on the bit—a sort of rider-incited bolting.

With this type of horse, or any horse that answers the forward control and then refuses the restraining control, forcing the rider to resist with the rein until the horse is over or behind the bit, the rider must resort to the direct rein of opposition, allowing the outside rein to advance while shortening the inside rein and forcing a lateral flexion of a horse's neck and a lateral displacement of the haunches.

In a short time, the rider will be able to easily effect a disciplinary full halt. In fact, he will find the horse yielding to the bit during the first half of the full halt. When this point is reached, a half halt, or even a slight check, will be all that is necessary to return the horse to a state of bit obedience.

The half halt is done exactly as the first half of a correctly executed full halt. The rider, "feeling" that the correct response has been effected and that the horse has regained its supple obedience to the bit, then ceases the halting action whether it be a full, half, quarter, or eighth halt.

While executing half halts, do not cease the halting action before the bit goes "completely through the horse," which simply means that it must affect the jaw, poll, neck, back, and all the joints of the rear legs, and that there must be a perceptible flexion of these parts.

Many students, upon graduating to the more advanced half halts, cease the halting action when only the jaw and poll have been affected. This will prevent development of any true bit obedience, as the horse will quickly learn to respond to the bit by false compliance of the jaw and poll. The legs of the horse, on which depend carriage, balance, and mobility, will evade the rider.

The half halt grows naturally from the full halt. If the half halt is unsuccessful, does not go through the horse, the rider is forced to continue the halting action and complete a full halt. If the full halt fails, the rider must resort to the direct rein of opposition, flexing and displacing laterally, the stiffened haunches. The relative response of the horse, in all cases, will determine the degree of necessary discipline.

26

Shortened Trot

When the horse has developed the necessary strength to remain nicely on the bit for relatively long periods at a vigorous trot, he is said to be at a working trot. (He must give the impression that he is working not loafing.)

While at the working trot, with the rider posting passively, the forward control will be applied in an attempt to lengthen the stride and, therefore, increase the forward rate while *remaining at the same timing.* The horse must remain in the same outline, except for stretching a bit more. He should be softly on the bit, supple, keep constant rhythm, and increase his stride.

When the stride has increased somewhat, within the framework of the horse's ability at the moment, we will attempt to shorten the stride, slowing the forward rate, while maintaining the added action we have created. If we are successful, the increase of stride, extension, will be converted into a higher action, and we will have achieved a shortened trot, which we will attempt to maintain only while slowing the rate to the original working trot. The time is not yet ripe to maintain the shortened trot to the point of collection, and overeagerness or greed will only frighten away the bird of collection.

In this on-the-bit work, the rider applies the forward control (balance forward and leg pressure), asking for a lengthening of stride. When the horse responds, the rider must continue the forward control while gently restraining the horse with his hands. If he were not to do so, the added action gained by extending the stride would be

138

lost, and not converted into a higher action. The horse would merely return to the working trot with no display of a more expressive trot. The rider should feel as if he were slowing to the original rate by shortening the stride—not the timing. The horse must continue to work as hard while slowing as he did while extending. The forward control must maintain the added engagement of the rear legs so that the horse slows on them, increasing their flexion and support, thus momentarily relieving more of the load from the forelegs. But, more importantly, the spark of animation, of life, must be awakened; the spirit and will to go forward and the desire to try for the rider must be created. The rider must be able to breathe life into his horse. No amount of purely mechanical control will enable the rider to achieve the shortened trot, a trot that will automatically become the collected trot.

In the beginning, we will ask for only a few steps of the shortened trot, being satisfied if the horse gives us an indication that he understood that which we asked by slowing the rate through a shortening of his stride, shifting more of his weight to his haunches, thereby lowering them, accepting the load on his flexed hocks in a soft cradling action, and, above all, remaining supple. Any tenseness at this time will absolutely prevent the horse from learning the shortened trot.

Tenseness may be caused by the horse being insufficiently obedient, having rear legs, especially the hocks, not strengthened enough by regular, gymnastic work, hard, disturbing seat and hands (seat, hands, and signals that do not breathe with the horse), an ill-fitting bit or saddle that causes discomfort, frightening or distracting occurrences (dogs in the arena, etc.).

The most common cause of failure to achieve the shortened trot is the rider's atempt to force a compliance to the controls. Only an obedient response to the restraining and forward control will leave the horse with the necessary freedom and suppleness to achieve the shortened trot.

If the horse manifests any disobedience, he must be reschooled in the natural gaits until he is obedient—only then may the on-the-bit work be continued.

There is no such thing as a disobedient collected horse. A collected horse is one that gives himself unconditionally to the rider; he willingly surrenders to the controls.

27

Relative Seat and Back Control

The rider's seat must correspond to the progress made by the horse, i.e., a seat that would be correct on a collected horse will be completely wrong on a partially trained horse.

As explained earlier, the normal balanced seat is achieved by standing in the stirrups on the balls of the feet, balancing, lowering the heels, and sinking straight down while maintaining this balance. If the saddle is correctly placed, and the seat-stirrup relationship is correct, the rider will be sitting erect, with his pelvis perpendicular over the lowest point on the horse's back—approximately the fifteenth vertebra. All seats are developed from this balanced seat. With the balanced seat, the bottom of the pelvis—the seat bones, rounded like the runners on a sled—is in direct contact with the saddle. We can, by leaning forward, shift our weight to the front edge of the seat bones, and more to the front of the horse, or, by leaning back, shift our weight to the rear of the horse (*see photo of human pelvis, page 20*).

If we lean forward, while keeping our back straight, on a stationary horse, the back muscles, activated to maintain us in this out of balance position, will apply an equal pressure, in addition to the forward weight shift, on the horse's back. This pressure, although slight, is the back control, and the horse can learn to respond to it. This back control pushes the saddle forward.

Weight shifted forward with active back control

Weight shifted forward, inactive back control

Weight shifted back with active back control

Weight shifted back, inactive back control

It is also possible to shift our weight forward without using the back control by allowing our pelvis to tip forward, arching the small of the back, the shoulders moving forward only slightly, until we are balanced on the front edge of our seat bones. In this case, we have effected a forward shift in weight, *without a back control*, preparatory to pressing the horse's sides with the calf of our legs and going forward.

We may also lean back, without bending our back, and shift our weight to the rear edge of our seat bones, and, of course, to the rear of the horse.

The muscles activated to maintain us in this out of balance position to the rear will also push the saddle forward and exert a back control.

Or we may rock to the rear edge of the seat bones by tipping our pelvis to the rear, slumping, our shoulders moving slightly to the rear, while *maintaining our balance, without a forward urging back control*, shifting our weight to the rear.

On a horse that is moving forward, if we lean forward only enough to remain in balance, the seat will be passive, a following seat, but also a balanced seat, for we now are in a dynamic balance with the forward movement.

If the rider shifts to the forward edge of the seat bones and shoves his seat forward, by bracing his back, attempting to stretch his seat in the saddle as if he would shove the saddle up the horse's neck, he is applying an active back control. The horse will learn, through the

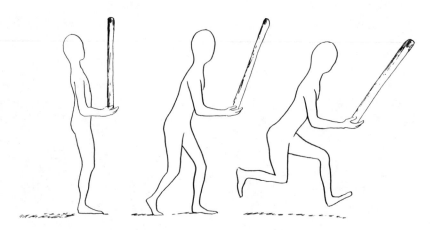

The balanced stick theory: The stick represents a balanced rider. This theory is valid until the horse enters a state of collection.

already learned use of the forward urging legs, to respond to this control.

The force against the horse's back is generated by the back muscles attempting to raise the weight of the leaning upper body. In this case, the weight and the degree of forward lean will determine the maximum amount of back control. But if the force of the clinging lower leg is added, the back control can be supplemented considerably.

If the rider leans back and shoves his seat forward in conjunction with the pull of his pressing lower legs, he will be using the strongest back control possible. This control is sometimes necessary on a runaway or a horse that refuses to answer the bit, but it should only be applied momentarily and never maintained for any length of time.

It can easily be seen that an infinite number of back controls may be applied. All riders use them correctly at least part of the time but to become a polished rider, one cannot rely on instinct or chance; one must learn to use his back with the same precision as the hands.

The rider has at his disposal five controls: voice, balance, legs, hands, and back. Not to use any one of these controls is to give away twenty percent of the control!

It can be seen that we have *two* separate controls available through the seat. We may use them separately, or in any combination. They may be used actively or passively.

The first control is felt by the horse as a shift of weight forward or backward in the saddle—it increases the load on the front or rear legs respectively. For example, the rider will use a *passive* weight shift forward to *follow* the forward motion of the horse in order to remain over the horse's center of balance. He may use an *active* weight control if he shifts his weight forward slightly ahead of the horse's center of balance, to indicate to the horse that he wishes to increase the forward rate. A passive shift of weight to the rear will enable the rider to remain in balance on a horse that slows unexpectedly or to follow the center of gravity as it moves to the rear as a horse increases his collection. An active shift of weight to the rear may be used to signal the horse to slow his pace, load the rear legs in the shortened trot or any collected gait, or anchor the seat when a strong rein action is necessary.

A combination of the active weight control and the active back control would be as follows: On a stationary horse, the rider shifts his weight forward by tilting his pelvis forward, his back inactive.

He then presses the horse's barrel with the calves of his legs. If the horse refuses to go forward, he may apply a stroke of the crop behind his leg to enforce the leg, or he may apply a strong forward urging back control before applying the crop, the latter usually being preferable, unless the rider is schooling the horse on the leg and weight control alone.

An active back control with a shift of weight to the rear (loading the rear legs) is used to slow the horse as in the shortened trot, to increase the horse's collection, or in a full halt or half halt (collected stops).

It should be used only for a moment at the proper time. If it is used too soon or maintained too long, it will overload the horse's loin and rear legs and cause his back to drop and his rear legs to drag behind.

Quite common among riders is the erroneous conclusion, "If I shift my weight to the rear and force the horse on the bit with a strong back, he will have to become collected." The riders that attempt this prefer to forget that *if force is necessary to maintain collection, the horse is not ready to be collected!*

The horse will learn, in time, to respond to the slightest of back signals through the use of the legs, and at times the leg signal will be unnecessary.

If the horse refuses to go forward in response to the back control, he must not be disciplined! The leg control must be used to enforce the back signal.

It is a sign of a willing horse, of learned obedience, when he goes forward in answer to the back control alone—he should never be forced to do so. There are many controls that a horse learns to obey indirectly, through other aids reinforcing them, and, upon a refusal, he must be disciplined through the original aids. His response to these advanced controls must be considered as a result of months of training—they cannot be forced! At a failure to respond, the horse must be returned to the original schooling exercise for the specific command.

For example, if an advanced horse refuses to go on the bit, he cannot be beaten or spurred into doing so. The specific underlying cause must be determined, and he must "be put back a few grades," so to speak, and retrained in the specific area of his resistance.

In any case, the rider's "feel" must tell him which seat or back control will be acceptable to the horse, determined by the horse's stage of development at the time. It is common, even in dressage competitions, to see riders using a recognized variation of the balanced seat that is inappropriate for the horse's development or actions.

An illustration might be a rider sitting erect, loading the horse's loin and rear legs, driving with the back, on a horse that has not engaged its haunches and is not collected.

The seat may be a good seat, one which the rider worked long and hard to learn, but it is out of keeping with the horse's stage of training. It is just as wrong although not as obviously as a rider using the forward jumping seat while riding the collected trot.

When the time comes for the rider to sit erect and use a forward-urging back control, the horse will invite him to do so by lowering his vigorously engaged haunches through increased flexion of the hip, stifle, and hock joints, while his forehand is relatively elevated. The rider will "feel" that there is no other possible way to sit comfortably with the horse.

People, in their endeavor to imitate the successful rider, invariably choose as their model an excellent rider on an *advanced* horse. This rider sits erect, his back slightly braced, or unobtrusively following the forward pulsations of the movement; he has a positive rein control on the bit, which the horse chews softly. He is correctly riding a collected horse.

But the novice, on his own or through the urging of a self-appointed riding instructor, imitates the seat on a horse that can as yet only carry him at the natural gaits, thinking that the seat will cause the horse's collection, and not vice versa.

The horse, his back and haunches not yet sufficiently strengthened, hollows his back and drags his rear legs behind in an effort to evade the pain of the overload.

This is not to say that the back and seat cannot be used *gradually* to influence a horse toward assuming a collected position. An excellent exercise for developing all the fine nuances of the back control is to straddle a stool of the appropriate height and squat to a seat with the leg position used when seated correctly on a horse. Lean forward and, without using the hands or legs or changing your forward inclination, tilt the stool forward with the back. Now slowly lower the stool until the rear legs are again in support; or with the rear legs raised, gently change the stool's inclination by use of the back alone.

It is well to end a discussion of seat and back controls with the reminder that, in the beginning of training, only the rider's legs can effect an engagement of the horse's rear legs.

28

Collected Trot to Extended Trot

In time, our horse will be able to maintain the shortened trot for longer periods. The rider will tactfully try to lengthen, to stretch out, the distance covered in slowing the more extended working trot, but never at the cost of a loss of timing or action or suppleness. We are not interested in slowing the rate in itself, but in increasing the carrying capacity and action of the haunches while slowing the rate.

When the joints and muscles of the rear legs have been suppled and strengthened sufficiently, through alternating from the working trot to a more extended stride and back to the original working trot, the shortened trot will become more supple and develop expression. It will have become the *collected* trot.

Let's take a look at the change in the action of the rear legs brought about by changing a horse from a *natural* gait to a *collected* one.

In the natural trot, a rear leg swings forward and grounds the hoof *ahead* of a plumb line through the base of support of the haunches. (The forward motion forces the horse to maintain a dynamic stability—the horse instinctively attempts to maintain its equilibrium.) After the hoof is grounded in support, it moves back and shoves off *behind* the plumb line through the base of support; the other leg then repeats the trot sequence.

When the horse is placed in a collected trot, his attempt to take a longer step is restrained by the bit. The step, unable to *extend*, is lifted *higher* before being grounded ahead of a plumb line through the center of support—but not as far ahead as in the natural trot. The leg then swings *back to*, or *slightly past*, depending on the degree of collection, the plumb line through the base of support and shoves off while the leg is in more of a flexed state than in the natural trot. The correlation of the degree of lift to the forward thrust will be determined by the degree of collection.

This action is felt by the rider as a soft cushioning, although springy, gait.

If we were to compare a human to a collected horse, the human would have to trot on continually bent knees and raise the knees higher, and thus he would spend relatively more time in suspension.

With this in mind, we can easily see the great strain placed on the horse's muscles and tendons by the collected trot, and, therefore, ask only for short periods at this gait until the horse is sufficiently strengthened.

To achieve the extended trot we place the horse in the collected trot, then ask for a lengthening of stride and allow the horse to stretch his head forward a little—all acceleration must be accompanied by a relative lengthening. We want to maintain our collection during the extension of stride. The horse should not use all of his collection in performing the extension, for then he has performed only a lengthened trot. It takes months or years to achieve a good extended trot, for it requires a tremendous stretching of the horse's muscles and tendons. The horse, at first, will not be able to extend his stride more than a little, even if he wished to do so. The reason for this is simple. To enter a collected trot the horse was first stretched. Then, maintaining this lengthened state, we bent him, greatly stretching his neck and back muscles, especially the muscles and tendons that pass over the croup and down the back of the rear legs. At this time in training, the horse is stretching to his maximum, but now we are asking for the extended trot, asking him to stretch his muscles even more in order to maintain collection while lengthening stride.

A true extended trot is a ground-covering gait, expressive, brilliant, collected.

29

Increasing Collection— Curved Lines and Circles

Once the working and collected trot have been achieved, we begin to work on curved lines in order to increase the carrying capacity of the horse's haunches.

Curved lines are an indispensable aid in the improvement of the horse's collection, for trotting or galloping on a curved line will, through the pull of centrifugal force, place a heavier load on the horse's inside legs, and particularly, since we have already increased the load on the rear leg through collection, on the inside rear leg.

If the horse is kept "straight" on the curved line, he must lean in slightly, thus being forced to raise his inside legs higher to clear the ground. His inside legs will follow the inside shorter track while his outside legs must follow the longer outer track. The outside legs, then, are forced to take a longer stride, and, with respect to the outer rear leg, increase its engagement further under the horse. Thus we have increased collection by increasing the load on the inside rear leg and by increasing the stride of the outside rear leg.

But there are pitfalls to be avoided while riding curved lines. The horse, when forced to follow a curve with too short a radius ridden at the working or collected trot, will evade the discomfort of the excess load on his inside rear leg's joints in different ways.

He may simply move his rear legs off of the track of the curve and move sideways, go crooked from right rear to left foreleg on a left turn, and overload his inside shoulder, become crooked on a turn, and fall heavily on the outside shoulder.

Some horses will attempt these evasions because of their contrary lazy dispositions, but many are forced to evade by being ridden through tight turns too soon.

While riding the horse through the corners at a natural trot during earlier stages of his training, we avoided making tight turns that would overload the inside rear leg and cause the horse to fall on his shoulder, either inside or out. The radius of the turn was limited by the horse's relative stage of training; if we insisted on a sharp turn, by forcing the horse with the direct rein, we forced him to fall on his inside shoulder.

For a turn to have value, the horse must be kept from overloading his forehand. Now that we have the horse in a state of "equestrian balance" at the working trot, we can begin to decrease the radius of our turns, remembering that we must never buy an "increase of turn" with the coin of "loss of engagement." *The horse must stay nicely on the bit.*

We begin by trying to pass through a corner a little more tightly. The rider shifts his weight to his inside seat bone simultaneously shoving it forward (a unilateral back control), his weight stretching his inside heel toward the ground. His legs apply a slight pressure, dominant inside leg at the girth, outside leg back slightly, to increase the forward stretch and impulsion of the horse. His outside shoulder, arm, and hand advance, allowing the horse's outside to stretch, while his inside shoulder, arm, and hand withdraw slightly as the horse's neck flexes to the inside. His hands then move together toward the inside, the inside rein directing the horse into the turn. The outside rein, with an *indirect leading rein*, indicates the turn, but more importantly, it presses the rein against the horse's neck on the outside. The horse will yield to this rein as he yields to the pressure of the outside leg, turning as well as flexing about the rider's inside leg (*see chapter 31*, second-degree flexion). If all these controls work in concert the horse will pass nicely through the corner.

Does this description of a correctly executed turn seem terribly complicated? Well, it is, and when you consider that a pirouette at the canter (a turn where the rear hooves mark time on the same spot as the horse pivots on them) is nothing more than a turn, although the ultimate pinnacle that a turn may reach, you will see that every turn you make can be taking you and your horse in that direction. After all, the only movements possible with a horse are go, stop, and turn. (No, I did not forget "back," which will be explained later.)

The desire in a rider to execute each movement, no matter how fundamental, as nearly perfectly as possible will eventually result in a well-trained horse.

Let me clarify a few of the terms you need to know to ride a turn correctly.

UNILATERAL BACK CONTROL

The unilateral back control is adapted from the bilateral back control that I have already discussed, the difference being that instead of stretching the seat forward by bracing each side of the back equally, the weight is shifted to the inside seat bone which is then pushed forward, the point of the hip (ilium) thrusting forward

Unilateral back control engaging rear leg during stop

slightly. This one-sided back control, along with the dominant inside leg pressure, engages the inside rear leg of the horse further onto a sustaining bit, increasing the collection and flexion. With the increased load, the engaged inside rear leg is flexed to a greater extent.

INDIRECT LEADING REIN

The first bit signal the horse learned was from the leading rein. He felt this signal predominantly on the corner of his mouth on the side to which he was to turn, but the signal passed through the bit and also applied pressure on the *opposite* corner of his mouth. So we had an inside direct bit pressure and an outside indirect bit pressure telling the horse which way to turn.

In a more advanced horse, due to the lighter direct signal of the leading rein, when using a training snaffle, there is little, if any, indirect pressure passed through the bit to the opposite corner of the mouth. In order to make the signals clearer to the horse, the rider must cause the outside rein to furnish this indirect bit pressure to the outside corner of the horse's mouth.

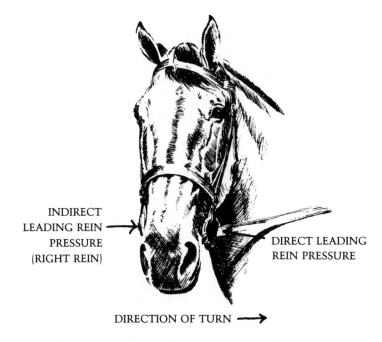

INDIRECT
LEADING REIN
PRESSURE
(RIGHT REIN)

DIRECT LEADING
REIN PRESSURE

DIRECTION OF TURN ⟶

Correct direct and indirect bit pressure during a turn

DIAGONAL NECK REIN SIGNAL

As well as yielding to an indirect leading rein, the horse must respond to an outside rein that is pressed against his neck.

Do I hear cries of "Heresy!" from the dyed-in-the-wool English riders? Then let me say, here and now, that correct "absolute" horsemanship does not depend on the style of saddle, tack, or riding employed. It makes not a particle of difference to the horse which style of saddle—English, Western, Mexican Charro, Arabian, Peruvian, Chinese, Russian, etc.,—is used as long as it is comfortable to the horse and rider and does not interfere with the principles of horsemanship. Which style of riding chosen is entirely a matter of personal preference. It is not uncommon in today's National Horse Show circuit to see many competitors showing one horse in both English and Western competitions at the same show. Sally Scott, of Lemon Heights, California, a past student of mine of whom I am justifiably proud, won in both English and Western classes at the gigantic and terribly competitive National Arabian Horse Show at Scottsdale, Arizona, and was subsequently chosen Junior Rider of the month by the *Arabian Horse Journal*.

SHOULDER-FORE EVASION

Inevitably, in the discussion of turning, the subject of "shoulder-fore" arises. Shoulder-fore is a legitimate two-track movement that will be discussed at greater length under that heading, but we are now concerned with a movement executed by the horse as a disobedience, an evasion of the controls.

As the horse will use the shoulder-fore position to nullify the bit in order to bolt, this vice must be vigorously attacked by the rider. The horse is using a shoulder-fore position (at times called a shoulder block) when he is flexed in one direction, but elects to follow his leading shoulder in the other.

The horse that has not been trained to respond to the outside rein pressing against his neck realizes that there is no restraining control in the direction of his outside shoulder, for the bit is now to the side and no longer effective, and evades the controls in that direction. He cannot evade straight ahead, for the bit prevents it. He cannot evade to either side, for the lateral leg control prevents it. He cannot evade to the rear by holding back, for the forward control prevents it. So he chooses the only "hole" open and bolts through it.

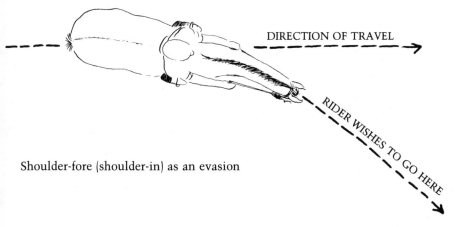

DIRECTION OF TRAVEL

RIDER WISHES TO GO HERE

Shoulder-fore (shoulder-in) as an evasion

The rider must be able to block this "shoulder-fore hole" with the outside rein pressure on the neck. This rein is called the "neck rein" by knowledgeable Western reinsmen who do not confuse it with the common neck rein wherein the rider's hand crosses the neck and applies pressure to the top of the neck, or still worse, tries to force the horse to bend his neck and turn.

Whenever I have a student who crosses the neck with his rein, pressing down against the crest, I ask him if he would like the horse to dig a hole. After he assumes a puzzled expression and asks "Why?", I explain that that is the direction in which he is trying to direct his horse. Trained horses yield to all pressures, so if a horse were to yield to a downward pressure, he would have to dig!

The hands must remain on their respective sides of the neck, for if they cross the center line of the neck, control of the rear leg on that side of the horse will be lost. The rein pressure to which the horse must learn to respond is felt by the horse on the side of his neck.

To teach a young horse to respond to the direct rein pressure on the neck, we merely apply the rein during a turn and tap the horse's shoulder with a crop. He will quickly associate the rein pressure with turning, and the touch of the crop will soon be unnecessary.

To retrain a spoiled horse and prevent him from a shoulder-fore evasion is another matter entirely.

The rider must go into a turn apparently naive, but thoroughly prepared, with the crop in the hand that is on the side to which the horse previously evaded. At the moment that the horse "bulls"

The neck rein

Reins in one hand to stop a
shoulder-fore evasion

through the neck-rein pressure, the rider should switch the reins to
one hand, and apply a few vigorous strokes of the crop to the shoulder that is going fore, while maintaining all the signals for the turn.
If the turn controls are stopped, the horse will not understand the
point of discipline.

Great care must be taken in the manner in which the reins are
held in one hand in order not to lose the proper rein on each side of
the horse's neck.

To be avoided at all costs is the instinctive shift of weight toward
the outside shoulder to which the crop is being applied. This faulty
shift of balance will indicate to the horse that the rider *wishes* to go
in the shoulder-fore direction.

The rider's crop hand must be able to work independently of his
body, which must maintain all the controls (balance, back, legs, and
reins) of the turn.

30

The Three Turns

A horse is relatively inflexible laterally in comparison to a dog. Due to the closeness of his ribs, he cannot easily bend to the side. His lateral flexibility can be improved by gymnastic training until he is capable of flexing his body to the circumference of a circle with a diameter of six meters (six steps, approximately twenty feet). A circle of this size is called a volte and is the smallest circle to which a horse can be flexed on one track. Due to the limit of his natural flexion, if he is forced to follow a smaller circle he must move on two separate tracks (in a sideways movement). A horse may also execute a volte by turning on the forehand or haunches, for an average horse's length is nine feet.

A stationary horse may be turned around in a number of ways: 1) the method of effecting a 180° change of direction that we use until the horse learns the turn on the forehand is the turn done by following a half circle, keeping the horse on one track, and keeping the half circle large enough so that it is easy for the horse to turn; 2) the horse may be turned about by pivoting on the forehand; 3) the horse may effect an about face by pivoting on the haunches; 4) the horse may turn about by pivoting over his center of gravity (*this type of turn is wrong and should not be practiced as a turn on the spot*—it is most frequently seen when a novice attempts to force a horse that is not yet ready to turn on the haunches); 5) and a horse may turn about by using any one of the above in combination. But for the turn

155

Voltes

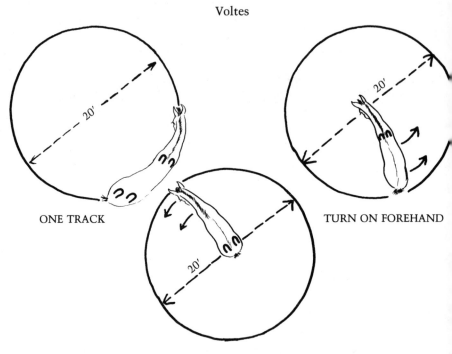

ONE TRACK

TURN ON FOREHAND

TURN ON HAUNCHES

to be "clean," the horse must either follow the half circle on one track, or execute a turn on the forehand or a turn on the haunches.

As a training exercise, a combination of these three turns may be used (a discussion of these exercises will be undertaken under two-track work), but in these exercises a simple change of direction is not the desired object.

In any case, it is well for the student to remember that a horse *cannot* turn about until his feet are placed in motion. It is as illogical to attempt to turn a stationary horse by means of the reins alone as it is to attempt to turn an automobile by twisting only the steering wheel.

31

First- and Second-Degree Flexions

Only a slight measure of flexion (bending the horse around the inside leg) is possible until a horse reaches the level where he responds to the diagonal controls and develops the balance of collection.

First-degree flexions are begun by flexing the horse with the leading rein and inside leg on the same side (lateral controls), the rein flexing the horse's neck and the leg flexing the horse at the ribs. The horse will have learned to flex to the inside leg during turns on the forehand.

Once the horse learns, by being repeatedly stopped from a lateral movement while executing the turns on the forehand, to respond to the outside leg (a left leg, for example, while moving to the left), and also to respond to the outside neck-rein pressure, through frequent use on the turns (a diagonal control), higher level first-degree flexions are possible—the outside controls exerting a holding action against the laterally moving action of the inside controls, thus insuring a flexion of the entire body.

Second-degree flexions are obtained by actively bending the horse, with the diagonal rein and leg, about the inside leg, which exerts the

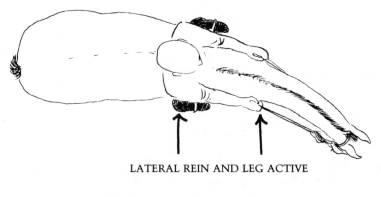

LATERAL REIN AND LEG ACTIVE

Beginning first-degree flexion

DIAGONAL CONTROLS HOLDING

LATERAL CONTROLS ACTIVE

Advanced first-degree flexion

holding action. They are the result of a horse responding obediently to a combination of learned signals. While a rider may force a first-degree flexion with the inside rein, it is impossible to obtain second-degree flexion by force.

If force is applied to the diagonal rein (neck pressure rein), the bit will be simultaneously pulled back until the horse stops or changes his flexion. If the crop or spur is used to force a flexion to the outside leg (diagonal leg), the horse will respond, thinking the leg is exerting a forward control by bolting forward.

32

Increasing Poise on the Small Circle

We will gradually begin to improve our horse's poise and suppleness at the working trot by decreasing the radius of our turns. This is done in two ways. First, we begin to decrease the size of the large circle (like the lunge circle, with a radius of thirty feet), making sure that the horse remains on the bit and straight. If the horse's timing should falter, we immediately ride him up to the bit on a straight line and regain his poise and engagement. Second, we begin to bend the corners of the arena more tightly.

When the horse has developed the necessary balance and suppleness to enable him to *bend* through a corner correctly and easily, with the arc of the circle at a ten-foot radius, the turn may be continued into a half circle.

When these two parallel lines of training mature and come together, the half circle in the corner may be increased to a full circle (volte).

The trainer will have to rely on his "feel" to determine how rapidly the horse may be pushed toward executing the small circle. If he becomes "greedy" to show a ninety-day wonder, the horse will lose his suppleness, his fluid gait and be forced to any number of evasions, as is, sadly, too often the case.

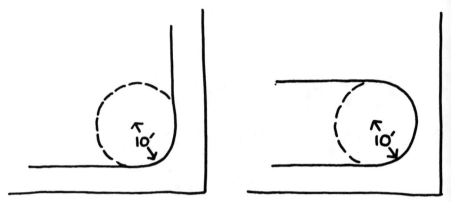

Increasing the arc of the corner to perform a half circle

When a self-appointed trainer, working without experienced help, tells me that he is training his horse, my mind automatically thinks, "Sure you are, but training him to do what?"

We must remember that we are always training a horse when we are working with him, training him for better or worse, but training him nevertheless. And only then will we come to realize that it is much more difficult to learn *what not to do* with a horse, what mistakes to avoid, than *what to do.*

Now that we can ride the horse at the working and collected trot on circles of a twenty-foot diameter, we continue at this work for a time, allowing the centrifugal force to load and strengthen the inside rear leg, being careful to keep the horse on the bit, and *in first position.*

33

Lateral Movements— Two Track, Shoulder-in

When a horse's rear hooves follow exactly his fore hooves, he leaves one track, the width of which will be measured by the distance between the outside edges of the hoofprints. This one track may be either on a straight or curved line, and the horse's body will be longitudinally flexed or straight to conform to the line of travel.

When a horse's rear hooves do not exactly follow the fore hooves, he leaves a double, or two-track line (if the track measures wider between the outside edges than the width of a normal one track, it is considered a two track).

This two track may be either on a straight or curved line, and the horse's body will not be longitudinally flexed to conform to the line of travel.

As previously discussed, two-track exercises are done to gain the necessary control for preventing the horse from moving crookedly on two tracks in an attempt to evade the rider's controls, for the same controls that can cause a two-track movement can prevent it in an opposite direction, by exerting a holding action.

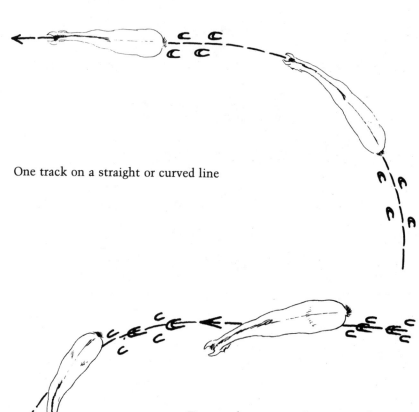

One track on a straight or curved line

Two track on a straight or curved line

Two-track exercises are also done to increase the rider's control over the longitudinal flexion of the horse's body and increase his flexion at the ribs (suppleness of back).

It is also possible to train a horse to be more maneuverable through two-track work—a turn on the haunches, for example, is a two-track movement.

Two-track training will make it possible for the rider to position and prepare his horse for a specific movement and thus insure its flawless execution.

Collection, too, may be improved by two-track exercises, although it is never caused by it, as is so often, and erroneously, believed. A horse may be put into collection while changing from a one-track to a two-track movement by being pushed forward (on the

bit) and restrained at the moment of assuming the two-track movement, but the resultant collection is *not* the result of the two-track
movement.

Once the horse has assumed some degree of collection, his collection may be increased by two-track exercises, for these exercises
are capable of increasing the load on the rear legs through moving
the haunches closer to the forehand.

All two-track work begins with the turn on the forehand, a
movement we began early in the horse's training to prevent lateral
evasions and establish a basis for future leg control.

The turns on the forehand in motion were refined into leg yielding, which enabled us to place the horse in *first position* and execute
more precise curved lines.

Leg yielding (a two-track exercise) to achieve first position is
done in the following manner.

When the inside leg control is reinforced by increasing the flexion
through inside rein, in an attempt to cause the horse to yield to the
leg and step sideways with his rear legs, the horse is forced to flex at
the ribs at the point of the rider's leg contact. When he flexes, preparatory to stepping sideways, his inside rear leg is automatically
placed laterally further under the weight toward a longitudinal me-
dian line of support. When this flexion of the ribs and the resultant
positioning of the inside rear leg is accomplished, the rider ceases to
ask for a lateral movement. He has gained his desired goal, flexion of
the ribs and *first position*, which enables him to ride through the
corner, or circle, correctly.

A short explanation of the different meanings of the term
"shoulder-in" is in order. A horse is executing a "shoulder-in movement" when he is flexed at the ribs and moving laterally to the
direction opposite his flexion. Any time a horse is flexed at the ribs
he has his shoulder "in," and he may be on one track on a curved or
straight line, or doing a "shoulder-in movement." In other words, a
horse performing a "shoulder-in," two-track movement must have
his "shoulder-in" while a horse on a curved line on one track will
also have his shoulder "in" but will not be performing a "shoulder-
in" movement.

To teach the horse shoulder-in, we begin at a collected trot, by
assuming first position while turning our horse toward the fence on
the long side of the arena. In the beginning, to make it easier for the
rider, we make this turn rather long so as to eliminate the possibility
of the horse moving his haunches away from the fence. *The horse*

must make a proper one-track turn toward the fence—he must follow his head. This moment is crucial, for if the horse moves his haunches away from the fence, he does a moving turn on the forehand, shifting his weight to the forehand and destroying any possibility of increasing the load on the haunches and thus achieving collection. The holding action of the outside leg must prevent this.

We ride our horse along, then, at a collected trot about ten feet from the fence on our left. We make a smooth turn toward the fence, assuming first position. When the horse reaches the fence, which, needless to say, must be high enough to prevent him from sticking his head over it, we increase the pressure on the horse's ribs with the calf of our inside leg simultaneously with shifting our hands to the right. Our seat adapts to the horse's left flexion while our weight follows the direction of movement; we sort of ride off over the horse's outside shoulder, on down the fence. The horse will take a few steps in shoulder-in, which will satisfy us for the moment, and we will straighten him and ride on.

But there are things that can go wrong. As previously mentioned, the horse may not turn but move his haunches out, falling on the forehand.

The rider may also make the turn too short and come to the fence at an obtuse angle, forcing the horse to move at such a lateral position that he finds it impossible to maintain his engaged haunches. The correct angle for beginning shoulder-in will have been assumed when the horse's inside rear hoof is tracking its outside fore hoof and this diagonal leg is following the straight line of travel.

There are horses that become confused at coming to the wall and lose their suppleness. These horses must be first introduced to the movement at a calm, natural (uncollected) walk. Once the required movement has been explained to them at the calm walk, the rider should have no difficulty with the shoulder-in movement at the collected trot.

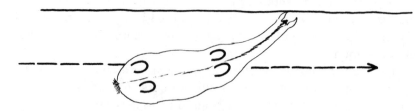

Left shoulder-in, head-to-wall, showing shoulder-fore position—the correct degree of lateral displacement for beginning the movement

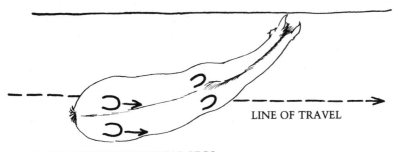

LINE OF TRAVEL

DIRECTION OF THRUST OF REAR LEGS

Incorrect shoulder-in, turned out at the hips

There are horses that seem to obey the inside leg and move easily to the side—*but without flexing at the ribs*. These apparently obedient horses are not obeying the lateral leg control, but are actually evading it. Through not flexing at the ribs, they are moving their haunches out of engagement.

In a shoulder-in movement the inside leg has two functions: to direct the horse to move to the side and to assist in flexion of the ribs, the essence of two-track work.

Horses that are exceptionally supple in the back manage to evade the beneficial effects of shoulder-in by excessive back flexion. They bend so much in the rib and loin that their rear legs continue moving in the original direction. This is called a *turning out* of the rear legs. With the thrust of the rear legs no longer directed toward the forehand, collection cannot be maintained, and thus the benefit of shoulder-in work—increasing collection—is lost.

In a correct shoulder-in, the rear legs must advance toward the forelegs, which are crossing, but should themselves step forward and to the side, as in first position, and never cross.

The lateral movement of the haunches is caused by the horse's positioned inside leg shoving the haunches and the raised outside leg to the side, not by the inside leg crossing under the belly in front of the outside leg. If the inside rear leg were to cross the outer leg, it would be impossible for it to support the weight of collection at such an angle.

There are riders who practice shoulder-in without collection and miss the point of the whole thing. They are doing the movement for the movement itself, having forgotten, if they ever knew, the purpose for doing a shoulder-in movement. Or perhaps they are practicing shoulder-in in order to comply with the letter of the requirement of a certain level dressage test, but they are not complying with the spirit of correct training—trying to advance the horse's collection through a series of gymnastic exercises.

Let's not forget the purpose of shoulder-in: to increase the suppleness of the horse's back through greater flexion at the ribs and the load on the rear legs, and consequently the collection, by moving the rear legs closer to the forelegs.

A certain degree of collection is necessary even to begin shoulder-in work, the exception being the brief introductory period at the walk where we are only interested in explaining what is required to the horse.

After a few steps in the shoulder-in along a straight line we swing the forehand away from the wall (a beginning turn on the haunches) back to one track, and straighten the horse in order to bend properly through the approaching corner. Care must be taken that the forehand swings away from the wall, back to the original line of travel, and that the haunches do not move toward the wall to the line of travel of the forelegs. This is done by relaxing the lateral pressure of the rider's inside leg, moving the hands further to the outside (during a left shoulder-in, head-to-the-wall), the outside, indirect leading rein directing the horse's forehand while the inside rein touches the neck, becoming a neck pressure signal that works in conjunction with the outside rein to swing the forehand, while the outside leg prevents the haunches from swinging out.

As the horse becomes more proficient at assuming a shoulder-in position, the size of the turn to the wall may be reduced appropriately, although we must always remain vigilant so that the haunches do not swing out and lose their engagement.

Returning the horse to one track from shoulder-in by swinging the forehand from the wall

When the horse can easily maintain a shoulder-in in one direction for the length of the arena, the exercise should be begun on the other hand and repeated until the horse is equally proficient on it.

SHOULDER-IN HAUNCHES-TO-THE-WALL

When head-to-the-wall shoulder-in can be done easily on either hand for the length of the arena, we will begin shoulder-in *haunches-to-the-wall* work.

We generally begin all new work to the left, for that is the easiest side for the average horse with a constrained left side. If we are working with the uncommon horse with the constrained right side, we will begin new work to that side, the reason being that we wish to make the initial learning period as easy as possible for the horse.

We begin left shoulder-in haunches-to-the-wall, at a collected trot, from the corner before the long side of the arena. We pass through the corner on the left hand, flexing the horse and assuming first position. We hold the turn until the horse's haunches comes to the long wall; then we hold the horse in this angle of displacement and continue down the wall of the long side of the arena.

The difficulty encountered in initial shoulder-in, haunches-to-the-wall work will be in restraining the horse with the bit, i.e., in preventing him from leaving the wall. Whereas in head-to-the-wall

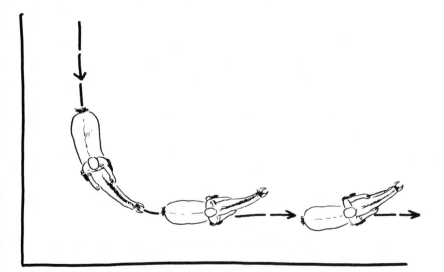

Beginning left shoulder-in, haunches-to-wall, from the corner

Left shoulder-in, haunches-to-the-wall

work, the wall prevented him from continuing on the arc of his turn, now the bit must take over this role; if it does not, he will merely cross the arena on a curved line.

In some cases, it is necessary to continue head-to-the-wall, shoulder-in work, gradually moving the line of travel farther from the wall until the psychological crutch of the wall is no longer needed. In this work, the rider rides down an imaginary wall that is one foot, then two feet, then three feet, etc., inside and parallel to the real wall.

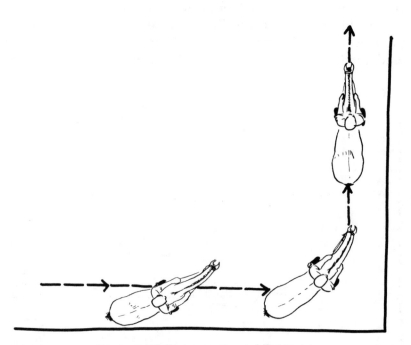

Returning to one track in the corner from a left shoulder-in, haunches-to-the-wall movement

Haunches-to-the-wall movements will work wonders at correcting the horse that swings out its haunches, as the wall now assists the rider's outside diagonal leg.

After going down one long side and reaching the corner, we return to one track, for to pass through the corner in a shoulder-in position at this point of training would wipe out any collection that existed.

When the shoulder-in, haunches-to-the-wall movement is done correctly, the original flexion, established in the first corner, will be maintained until the horse passes through the next corner.

To return to the one track in the corner, the rider moves his hands and balance to the inside and relaxes the lateral directing pressure of his inside leg. His inside rein now leads the horse into the turn with the aid of the outside neck rein pressure.

When the horse can go completely around the arena, in the left shoulder-in, haunches-to-the-wall except for the corners, where he is allowed to return to one track, he is ready to begin the right shoulder-in, haunches-to-the-wall work and continue it until he is equally proficient on the right hand. While performing a haunches-to-the-wall shoulder-in the rider should be able to leave the wall at any time, returning to one track on a curved line that corresponds to

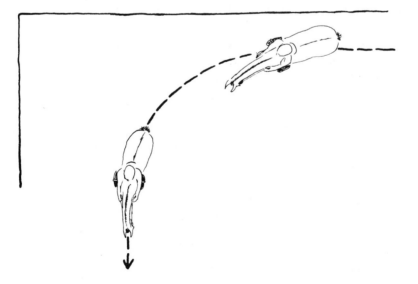

Leaving the wall from left shoulder-in, haunches-to-the-wall

Faulty head position in shoulder-in: head twisted and outside ear lowered

the horse's flexion. The previous work of returning to one track in the corner will have established the basis for this movement.

If the horse begins to drag and lose impulsion during shoulder-in movements, the rider should recapture the lost impulsion by riding vigorously forward on one track. Riding on two tracks for too long a period will quickly tire the rear legs, causing a loss of their elastic springiness, and have the opposite effect to that desired. Consequently, two-track work must be frequently alternated with freer movements.

One fault that frequently creeps into two track work is the horse twisting his head, lowering his outside ear, in order to free himself from the inside rein. This fault cannot be cured by increasing the outside rein pressure, as this would destroy impulsion and gait. The correct inside bit pressure may be restored by the application of a strong driving and guiding pressure of the rider's legs, forcing the horse to stretch and come to the bit.

As the horse's collection improves, we will gradually increase the degree of lateral displacement of the forehand that we ask for in shoulder-in.

The maximum degree of lateral displacement, for this level of training, will have been reached when the center line of the forehand is one step (approximately thirty-two inches) to the inside of

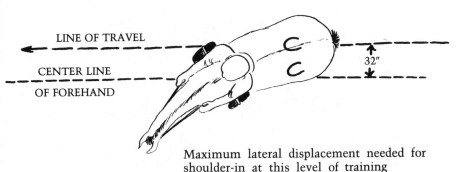

LINE OF TRAVEL

CENTER LINE

OF FOREHAND

32"

Maximum lateral displacement needed for
shoulder-in at this level of training

the print of the outside rear hoof. Lateral displacement in excess of
this will harm the action and collection, although greater lateral
displacement may be demanded, for short periods, of a highly trained
horse.

A further improvement in the horse's collection may be brought
about by practicing full halts in the shoulder-in.

During this movement the horse, his haunches already engaged
and brought even closer to the forehand by increased lateral flexion,
thus carrying a greater share of the load, is obliged to load his rear
legs even more. The hocks must bend more deeply during the short
moment of stopping. The horse's rear legs, acting like shock absorb-
ers, will be further strengthened, especially the large, powerful
haunch muscles, increasing the carrying capacity so necessary for
the cradling action of further collection.

The full halt during the shoulder-in movement must be performed with no loss of timing—the horse's rhythm, energy, and
collection *must not run down*, though there might be a slight increase in collection.

The rider asks for an increase of stride as the horse's diagonal leg
shoves off. During the ensuing phase of flight, he accepts and restrains this increase of impulsion, further engaging the haunches,
and lands the horse at a full halt, his back, legs, and hands working
in concert to bring about a fluid, soft, collected halt in the shoulder-
in. When the horse is completely halted, the rider must slowly relax
his restraining rein, back, and legs. The horse must relax and become uncollected, without moving his rear feet back. If the rider
maintains the strong controls that were necessary for the halt, the
horse will be forced to back, or step back with his rear feet while
simultaneously hollowing his back, in order to relieve the excessive
and painful load on his hocks.

171

34

Travers and Renvers, Second Position

Travers is a two-track movement that naturally evolves from its parent, the shoulder-in, the difference being that the horse is now traveling in the direction of his flexion, which is away from the wall. His outside rear hoof must step ahead and in front of his inside rear hoof while his fore hooves cross.

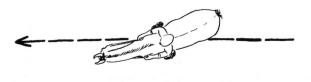

Travers

Both travers and renvers require that the horse be placed in *second position* before beginning the movement. In *second position*, the horse's inside rear hoof tracks the inside fore hoof, while the outside rear hoof tracks one-half a hoof's width inside the outside fore hoof.

Second position may be assumed on straight or curved lines. An observer standing directly in front of the horse will see one-half of the outside rear hoof between the fore hooves.

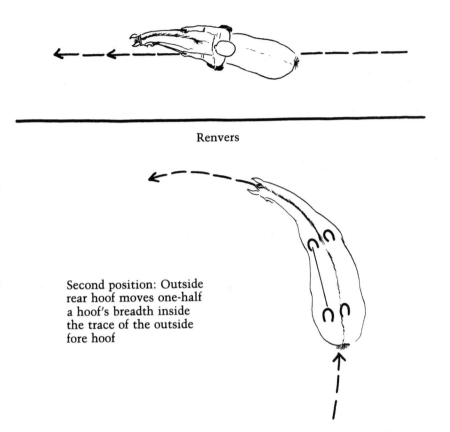

Renvers

Second position: Outside
rear hoof moves one-half
a hoof's breadth inside
the trace of the outside
fore hoof

This position is called the "flexed straight" position, for the horse
is slightly flexed, but "straight" in that he is flexed to the path he is
following and is evenly loaded on all four legs. His flexion is such
that the outside corner of his inside eye, or edge of his nostril is in
line with his shoulder and hip line.

A horse must respond to second degree flexion before he can be
placed in second position. The rider must be able to bend the horse
about his inner leg with the outside neck rein pressure and the
outside leg (diagonal controls). The horse must respond willingly to
these controls, as any use of force would destroy suppleness and
collection.

The horse's work in turn on the forehand, turning corners and
circles, returning to one-track from shoulder-in, preventing shoulder-
fore evasions, and shoulder-in yielding to the inside leg has prepared
him for second-degree flexion.

Second position: Eye, shoulder, and hip in alignment and traveling straight

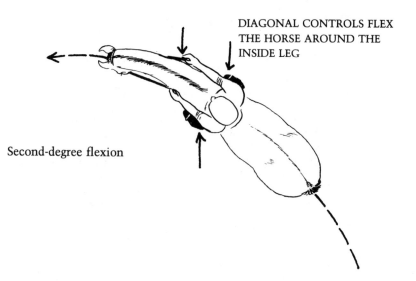

DIAGONAL CONTROLS FLEX
THE HORSE AROUND THE
INSIDE LEG

Second-degree flexion

To achieve second position in order to work on travers, then, we ride into the corner at a collected trot and bend the horse around our left leg with the outside rein and leg. When the degree of lateral displacement of the horse's forehand, as his head comes to the wall, aligns his inside fore hoof with his outside rear hoof on the line of travel, we continue down the long side of the arena.

If the horse has difficulty maintaining the flexion in the direction of travel, if his collection begins to suffer, do not force the flexion, but allow him to change to a shoulder-in, head-to-the-wall in order to maintain his timing, stride, and collection.

Travers is a difficult movement for the horse to master, for he must respond to the laterally directing *diagonal leg*, a response that is a result of a trained horse responding to the leg which before was a lateral directing *inside leg*, a response that cannot be forced.

Great tact and patience in the rider are required to bring the

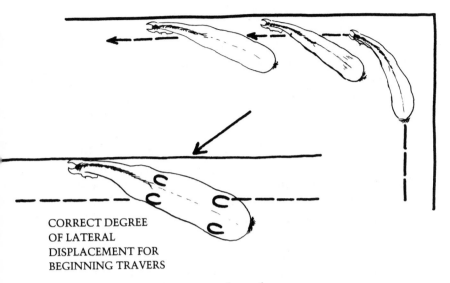

CORRECT DEGREE
OF LATERAL
DISPLACEMENT FOR
BEGINNING TRAVERS

Assuming travers from the corner

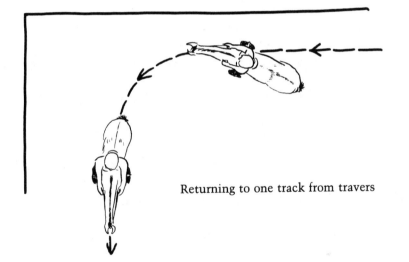

Returning to one track from travers

horse successfully through this crucial moment. Therefore, we allow the horse to learn the travers step by step, from the corner,
gradually increasing the number of steps as his ability increases,
returning to shoulder-in if the action begins to falter.

When the horse has gained the increased suppleness and collection necessary to maintain the travers for the length of the long side
of the arena, we cease to exert lateral controls and pass through the

corner on one track. To prove our control in travers, we must always be able to return to a curved line on one track.

When we are satisfied with the travers on the left rein, we begin the work over from the beginning on the right rein.

When the horse is equally proficient in the travers on either side, his lateral displacement not exceeding the point where his diagonal leg (inside fore, outside rear) is aligned with the line of travel, we begin work in the renvers.

Renvers, a more difficult position to assume than travers, is begun by riding close to the wall on our left side, at a collected trot. We take second position and swing the forehand away from the wall with our inside leg and rein while bending the horse and increasing the flexion by holding with our outside neck-rein pressure and outside leg.

In this movement, it is important that the forehand moves *away* from the wall to a new line of travel, and that the haunches do not move *toward* the wall. If the movement is begun close enough to the wall, the wall will help prevent this evasion. This evasion, this cutting in of the haunches is an attempt on the part of the horse to evade engagement and collection.

As in shoulder-in and travers, when the diagonal leg (inside fore, ouside rear) is aligned to the line of travel, the lateral displacement will be correct.

As in shoulder-in haunches-to-the-wall, the psychological support of the wall at the horse's head is missing in a renvers movement, so an increased obedience to the bit and leg is required to prevent the horse from leaving the wall.

In renvers and travers, the laterally moving control will be the outside leg. And as this is a *diagonal* control, it will be difficult, if not impossible, for the horse to accept it without true collection.

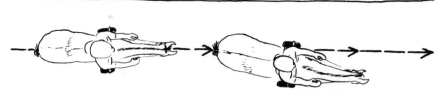

Assuming renvers and second position by swinging the forehand from the wall

35

Two-Track Exercises

Once travers and renvers are firmly established in the horse, a variety of two-track exercises are possible to increase his finer response to the controls and collection.

For example, we can, while maintaining the same degree of flexion, change from a travers to a shoulder-in after passing through the corner on one track. This movement, through the change in the lateral directing leg, sharpens the horse's leg responsiveness.

We can improve the horse's ability to go straight forward on one track from two track (a necessary movement to insure that the horse's collection does not flag as he begins to step more to the side than forward) by frequently executing one-track voltes from the travers.

We can ride completely around the arena, maintaining a constant flexion, alternating from travers to shoulder-in to travers through one track in the corners.

While riding down the short side of the arena, we can place the horse in second position and ride him in a travers away from the wall, down an imaginary diagonal wall that reaches from the center of the short wall to the center of the long wall.

This traversal displacement is known as half pass and, after a short period of familiarization, it may be ridden diagonally across the arena from the corner before the long wall to the opposite corner.

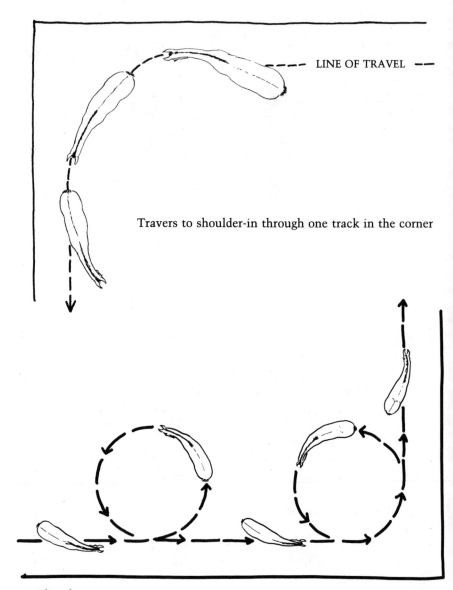

LINE OF TRAVEL ——

Travers to shoulder-in through one track in the corner

Voltes from travers

We should always be careful to keep the forehand leading the haunches.

In time, the degree of traversal displacement, the angle at which the arena is crossed, may be increased until the horse comes to the

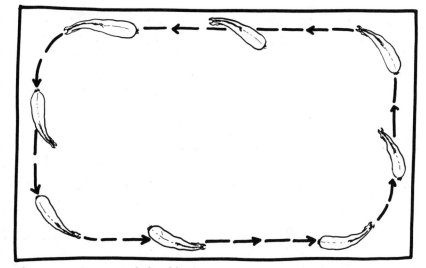

Alternating travers and shoulder-in

Beginning traversal

opposite wall before the corner where a change of position (flexion) is executed. This movement is a diagonal change of hand. The change of flexion and direction must occur when the horse comes to the wall, where the horse, for a time, must be ridden on a straight line.

Gradually, this straight line of travel may be shortened until it is nonexistent, except in the horse's mind, and a *double diagonal change of hand* may be ridden. For this movement the arena should be at least seventy by one hundred feet.

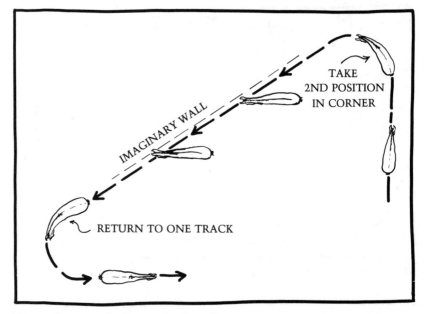

Diagonal traversal of arena (half pass)

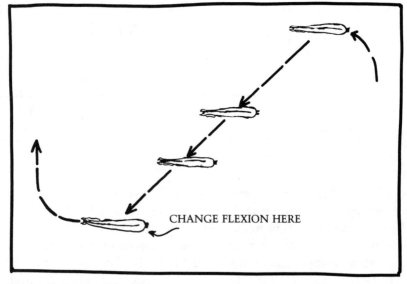

Diagonal change of hand

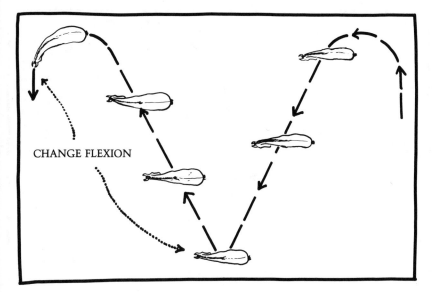

CHANGE FLEXION

Double diagonal change of hand

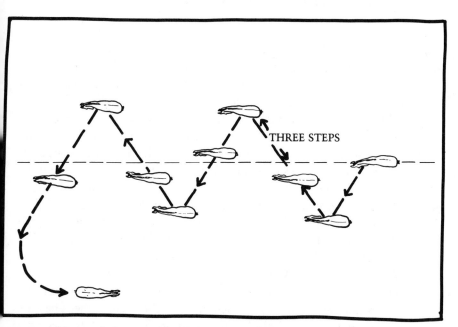

THREE STEPS

Zigzag (diagonal change of hand from the center line)

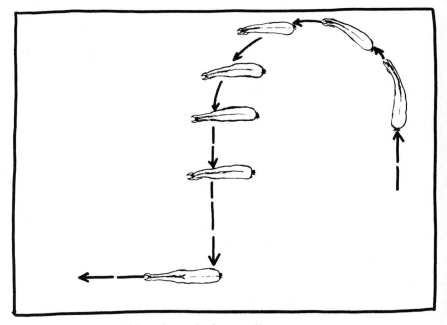

Traversing a curved line from the long wall

This exercise in turn can be elaborated: Working off of the center line of the arena, we advance to triple and quadruple *diagonal changes of hand*, commonly called "zigzag."

This movement is ridden with an equal deviation of three steps to each side of the center line. Great care must be taken that the horse does not lose his balance and stagger through the changes of hand, and that he stays erect and does not lean toward the direction of movement—he must be ridden at an expressive collected trot.

When the horse has developed the poise and balance and fine response to the controls necessary for multiple changes of hand, we can begin curved lines in a travers, the only manner in which the load on the inside rear leg may be increased.

We begin this work by riding a curved line from the long wall, keeping the curve as gradual as possible, to make it easy for the horse. By gradually increasing the degree of the turn, we will be able to complete a traversed circle the width of the arena. This we will gradually reduce in dimension until the horse is executing a volte.

Simultaneously we introduce the horse to a *turn on the haunches*.

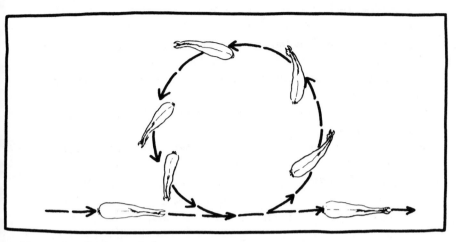

Traversing the large circle

We begin by riding the horse directly into a corner and stopping. We position the horse for a left turn, apply the forward control and direct the horse, as in a travers, for a left turn. The horse, seeing that he must either turn on his haunches or back, which is not a natural movement, will take a couple of walked steps of the turn on the haunches, until his head clears the fence and he can move straight forward. To further explain the desired movement to the horse, a few light taps of the crop on the outside shoulder are sometimes necessary.

When the horse understands what is required of him, we take him from the corner and repeat the exercise. Again we walk the horse, stop in a position for a left turn, and walk the horse through

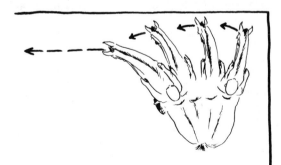

Beginning a turn on the haunches from the corner

a quarter turn to the left, ending by moving straight ahead on one track.

Now, as always when leaving the moral support of the wall or fence, the horse must become more bit obedient.

The turn on the haunches is a *forward movement,* and to be done correctly, the rear legs must be put in action before the turn is begun. In the beginning lessons, however, we allow the horse to pivot on inactive rear legs in order to calmly explain the new requirement. But soon we must force the horse to turn with the active rear legs maintaining the rhythm before he forms the habit of pivoting on dead rear legs and, consequently, falls heavily on the bit.

We position the horse for a left turn at the walk and do a partial halt, only enough to engage the rear legs and to change direction, making certain, with a strong forward control, that the rear legs continue the timing of the walk.

In these beginning turns, we willingly allow the horse to move forward a little, his rear hooves walking a smaller circle than his fore hooves, in order to maintain the impulsion and timing, though eventually we want the horse to turn without moving forward.

When we have completed a quarter-turn, we finish, as always, by riding the horse straight forward.

Through conscientious daily work, the horse should soon be able to do a half-turn with the active rear legs tracing a circle as small as three feet in diameter.

When this point is reached, we will begin to use the half-turn on the haunches to change direction on the perimeter of the arena. This exercise is an aid to most horses, for it gives them a practical reason for the movement.

To further improve the turn on the haunches and, consequently, the collection, through increasing the carrying capacity of the rear

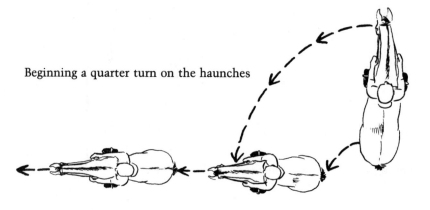

Beginning a quarter turn on the haunches

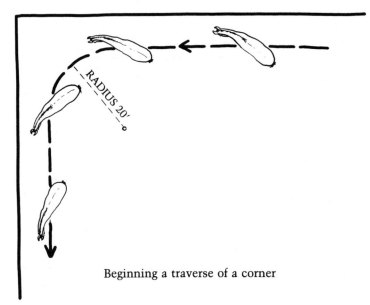

Beginning a traverse of a corner

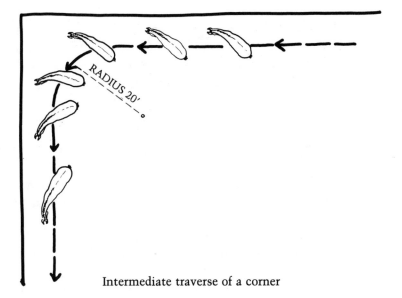

Intermediate traverse of a corner

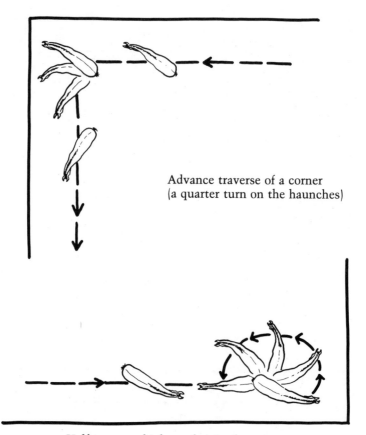

Advance traverse of a corner
(a quarter turn on the haunches)

Half turn on the haunches in the corner

legs, we will begin to traverse the corners of the arena at the collected trot.

In beginning this movement we round the corner into a quarter volte, maintaining the rate and timing and degree of lateral displacement.

Gradually, we will increase the lateral displacement, as in a traversed curved line, and finally we shorten the radius of the circle until we are performing a quarter-turn on the haunches at the collected trot. We have reduced the forward rate of the haunches to almost nothing while maintaining the rate with the elevated forehand. In this work we must pay strict attention to the action, engagement, and timing of the rear legs. We must not push for turning

Half turn on the haunches on the long wall

Turn on the haunches on the center line (gradually remove the horse from the wall)

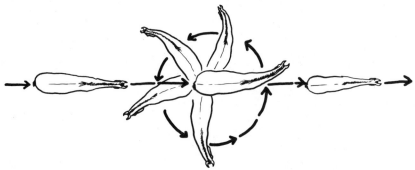

Pirouette at the collected trot

traversal quarter circle into a turn on the haunches at the expense of collection. Upon completion of the quarter-turn on the haunches through the corner, we continue on one track in second position.

In time, by patiently allowing the horse to develop the strength and carrying capacity of his haunches, we will be able to increase the quarter-turn into a half-turn, an about face, and return down the long wall on one-track.

Up to now, we have been entering the corner in a travers position. Now, as a logical step in progression, we will begin the half turn in the corner from one track in second position.

When the horse can easily execute a half-turn on the haunches, with no loss of timing, the action and lofty elevation of the freed forelegs having increased considerably, we can begin our half-turn *before* reaching the corner, and gradually, through beginning our turn at increasing distances from the wall, wean our horse from the moral support of the corner.

Now we are concerned with removing from the horse's mind the support of the long wall; so, we gradually ride parallel lines at ever-increasing distances from the wall, until we can execute a turn on the haunches from the center line at a collected trot.

When our horse has become proficient in this movement, we will increase our turn to a three-quarter-turn, and finally, to a full-turn—a pirouette at the collected trot.

A horse in a pirouette, in order to be completely in control, must be able to return to a straight line of travel at any time. The rider must take care that he does not get carried away with the exhilaration of the movement and pirouette the horse until he becomes dizzy, thus losing his confidence in the movement.

36

Work at the Gallop

We previously allowed our young horse to carry us at a gallop when he offered, through an excess of good spirits, to do so. As the horse had not yet developed the strength or poise, we refrained from *asking* him to gallop, although we let short gallops slip in occasionally before he was capable of a small degree of collection at the trot and travers work. When this point is reached (traversal at the collected trot), we can seriously began gallop training.

We begin on a circle, on the left hand, at a working trot. We assume second position, for it is from this position that a gallop depart can be most precisely taken, and *decrease* the size of the circle with a travers movement by use of the lateral-directing outside leg and outside rein, shifting our weight to our inside seat bone. When the circle is somewhat smaller, we enlarge it in a shoulder-in movement by switching to an inside leg pressure and outside rein, a rein which moves away from the neck and becomes an *indirect leading rein*, keeping our seat on our inside seat bone, but following the direction of movement with our weight. When we reach the original circle, we stop the lateral shoulder-in movement with the *outside* leg and neck-rein pressure.

In order to stop his outward movement, the horse will automatically shorten the stride of the outside rear leg, placing it in a gallop depart position. At this moment, we increase the *inside leg* pressure, lift the inside rein slightly, apply a strong forward-back control, and give the oral command to canter. It is very important that the horse canters from the inside leg and does not anticipate the movement and canter from the outside leg.

We use the oral command and the slight lift on the inside rein because these allow us to take advantage of the horse's earlier lunge training, thus making the desired response unmistakably clear to the horse.

A horse placed in a gallop in this manner cannot fail to take the correct lead—unless he is not responsive and takes one extra step before galloping, or unless he has a decided distaste for the lead in question and anticipates the command, taking the gallop one stride early. But if he is truly collected, he will not attempt these evasions, for he has given himself over to the rider. For these reasons, we have waited for collection before attempting gallop work, for no horse can be truly responsive until he is collected. A large percentage of the attempted movements will always fail with an uncollected horse.

The gallop depart may also be taught in the corner in the following manner. At a collected trot, we enter the corner before the long

Gallop depart from second position

side of the arena in second position. In the turn, we apply the command for a gallop as described above. Care must be taken with this method that the same corner is not used repetitiously, causing the horse to anticipate the command.

The major disadvantage with the corner depart, which is very similar to turning the horse from the long wall for a gallop depart, is that it is very difficult to prevent the horse from *cutting in* his haunches, a fault that invariably crops up in gallop work and is difficult to control, and a fault that renders further training at the gallop impossible. The gallop from the shoulder-in quite naturally eliminates the *cutting in* problem through the previously established control of the haunches with the inside leg.

In any case, whether from the circle or the corner, the rider must continue initiating the canter with the oral command and the slight lift of the inside rein until the horse is obedient to the commands. Eventually the rider can eliminate the oral command, but should retain always, the imperceptible lift of the inside rein. This must be done to eliminate confusion in the horse's mind when very similar controls are applied that *do not* call for a gallop depart.

The rider must also remain vigilant that the slight inward flexion of the neck is maintained, for the neck-to-shoulder-muscle that lifts the lead foreleg is rendered inactive by the outward flexion used by so many of the so-called "rapid trainers." These malpositioned horses will always gallop heavily on the leading foreleg.

Let's take a closer look at this type of gallop depart if only for the reason that it is the most common method in practice—and the most incorrect!

In this method, usually done from the trot in the initial stages, the rider pulls the horse's head to the wall while simultaneously throwing his weight away from the wall in an effort to unbalance the horse (all correct training is aimed at increasing the horse's balance). At the same moment, he kicks the horse in the belly on the inside (a kick in the belly causes the abdomen muscles, the muscles necessary for pulling the rear legs forward, to spasm and become ineffective). In response, the horse (he can't run away, for the wall is in his face) throws out his outside forefoot, in a falling motion, for the neck-to-shoulder muscle is rendered inoperative by his faulty flexion, in an instinctive effort to maintain his equilibrium, falling heavily on his lead leg (outside fore) and into a heavy-on-the-forehand gallop (his haunches were disengaged with the first pull of the rein)

Second position gallop depart from the corner

in which he gallops along crabwise, forever prevented from a correct gallop as long as this position is maintained.

François Baucher, nineteenth-century trainer at Saumar and the greatest trainer of his day, nevertheless believed in one glaring fallacy: he practiced the gallop depart in this manner, although in his book, *Methode d'Equitation*, he says, ". . . after the gallop is secured, *regain the horse's balance* and continue in a *normal manner*." "Regain the balance" is the key phrase, for it is definitely detrimental and quite unnecessary to interfere with a horse's balance unless he is intentionally defiant and willfully disobedient. And even if he is allowed to regain the correct gallop, he would still be unnecessarily learning the incorrect gallop, an impure gait that is better left unlearned.

This type of gallop depart is popular, for it enables the rider to

Correct gallop depart, horse flexed toward the lead

Incorrect gallop depart, horse flexed away from the lead

evade the necessity of learning the "feel" of the proper timing and foot position for a correct gallop depart—a feel that every serious horseman should know. Thus, in his hurry to force the horse into a correct lead, he cheats himself out of learning a valuable lesson. Also, by practicing faulty gallop departs, he prevents the horse from learning the hoof and leg position and collection that are necessary to his further advanced education.

There is a proper moment, when a horse's feet are in the right position, for the application of *all* commands. Applying a control when the horse's feet are in a position that makes it impossible for him to respond, besides ruining the horse's responsiveness (for he must wait for the proper moment before executing the command) destroys the horse's respect for the rider's intelligence, encouraging him to attempt disobediences.

A horse of good disposition that gallops in an unconstrained manner will naturally take second position. His outside rear leg, which supports the whole load upon landing after the suspension stage, will endeavor to seek a position laterally under the weight in compliance with his instinct to maintain equilibrium. This is the second reason for assuming second position prior to the gallop depart, and for maintaining it in all future gallops. Thirdly, there are horses that, after galloping a short distance, fall heavily on the forehand and spread their rear legs. This evasion of a correct gallop can be prevented by sustaining second position.

There is a common method of signaling a horse for a gallop with the rider's outside leg. This method has many disadvantages. First, the use of the rider's outside leg for a gallop depart will make it completely impossible to straighten a crooked trot or walk wherein the horse swings his haunches out; execute any travers movements at the walk or trot; straighten the horse at the gallop (a horse at the gallop on one track must be in the "flexed straight" position on straight or curved lines).

There are a number of reasons for not signaling a depart from the outside leg. First, if we attempt to straighten a crooked horse—a horse that has been trained in this manner—at the walk or trot with the outside leg, he will gallop.

Second, if we attempt a travers movement at the walk or trot, the horse will gallop.

Third, if we try to straighten a galloping horse who is cutting in his haunches, he will attempt to change leads.

We will have purposely created an insurmountable obstacle to the horse's further training.

For the above reason, it is best to train the horse to gallop from a shoulder-in with pressure from *both legs*, the inside (dominant) leg pressing more strongly at the girth, the outside leg slightly back, as naturally positioned by the horse's flexion, vigilantly insuring that the horse stays on one track and that the haunches do not swing out.

A spirited horse may be incited into a fast gallop in the initial stages. With such a horse, do not attempt to forcefully slow him, for you will be teaching him to stiffen his neck, back, and rear legs against the bit. Instead, go along with the fast gallop, even encouraging the horse faster. Then, after he has worn himself down somewhat, now willing and not stiffening to the controls, gradually slow the gallop. Of course, a large arena, one that does not necessitate sharp turns at the extended gallop, is necessary for this work.

With a horse that continues to bolt after a gallop depart, gallop only for a few strides, which will be calm enough; then return to a calm walk through the trot.

A stiff charging gallop can also be easily controlled by placing the horse in a shoulder-in movement (inside rear hoof tracking the outside fore).

Repeatedly returning to the walk will progressively encourage the horse to gallop calmly for increasingly longer periods.

On the other side of the coin, we have the lazy horse whose gallop, after a few strides, seems to literally "fall apart."

Immediately, when the horse begins to lose the freshness and springiness of his stride, the rider must ride vigorously forward. This type of horse must know unconditionally that *leg means forward!* He may slow to an ordinary gallop only if he retains the fluid springy action of a correct gallop; at the first sign of faltering, he must be ridden forward energetically. Soon, he will learn that the forward control may also mean to improve his carriage.

In all attempts to achieve a specific lead in a gallop depart, the most important factor, and the most often ignored, will be the time, in relation to the horse's steps, at which the gallop signal is applied.

For example, a horse will always take the lead that corresponds to his foot position at the moment of depart. At the trot, the signal must be applied a split second before the outside rear leg (dominant leg in the first phase of the gallop) is grounded. This is the leg that, by being grounded sooner and shoving off strongly, breaks up the previous diagonal action of the trot. But the gallop signals cannot be given as the leg is grounded, for this would not allow the horse reaction time, and an allowance for reaction time must be considered, in relation to foot position, for all movements. This split second of lag between the application of the control and the horse's response, no matter how responsive the horse, will always be present. In other words, the rider must begin his signal immediately after the beat previous to the beat from which the horse responds.

If the rider has not yet developed sufficient skill to feel the proper moment to apply his control, he should practice gallop departs from the posting trot on an older, well-trained horse.

A gallop depart at the posting trot would be effected as follows: While posting the correct diagonal (sitting the inside rear and outside fore) at the working trot, the rider returns to the saddle, but instead of rising again, remains seated for an extra beat, exactly as in a change of diagonal. Between these two beats, the gallop control must be applied, signaling far enough ahead to allow for reaction time, for the horse to ground his outside rear leg sooner and shove off into a gallop, leading with the inside foreleg. With enough practice, the rider will soon be able to feel the exact moment for signal application at the sitting trot. He will feel the diagonal beats and choose the same moment as he did when posting.

It goes without saying that the type of precise work undertaken at the gallop demands a high degree of affinity between the horse and rider.

Before this point is reached, the horse will probably take the undesired lead many times. I purposely used the word "undesired" in place of "wrong" for, to a horse, there is no such thing as a wrong lead. There are preferred leads in that the horse will feel as if he were galloping "left-handed," so to speak, when placed in the infrequently used lead, and, although the lead will always depend on the foot position prior to the gallop, the horse may elect to wait a beat for a preferred lead.

If the rider finds himself in a gallop with an undesired lead, he must not, on any account, stop abruptly or discipline the horse in any way. To do so would cause the horse to think that to gallop is a mistake, and he would develop a permanent tense aversion to the gallop. Therefore, the rider must continue to gallop for a short period before gently and calmly returning to the trot. The rider asked for a gallop, and the horse gave him a gallop, the leading leg being completely irrelevant to the horse at this point. To discipline the horse will certainly tell him that to gallop is wrong!

Again, as in gallop departs on the lunge, the horse must be allowed the necessary time to learn and develop the skill and balance for a smooth gallop depart.

As the strength of the haunches develops, the horse will be able to gallop comfortably for longer periods, although at the first sign of discomfort, he must be returned to the trot, until finally, he can gallop completely around the arena. The easily rounded corners will present no difficulty, for he learned to gallop on a curved line on the lunge circle. He should never be galloped until he is tired, for even the horse with the gift of natural action will "fall apart" (fall heavily on his joints and lose the fluid springy action of a correct gallop) if galloped beyond his ability.

The horse, after developing the strength and suppleness to gallop effortlessly for long periods, will discover the natural collected gallop, as he did on the lunge, but now with the added weight of the rider.

When the horse has gained the ability to gallop in natural collection, we will begin to school him on the gallop depart from the walk. Before the rider can successfully attempt gallop departs from the walk, he must have a thorough knowledge of the horse's action at the walk and *be able to feel when each hoof is grounded.*

It has been my experience with students that, when asked to count cadence at the walk (left, right) with the grounding of the rear hooves, they invariably feel the hooves in reverse. In order to acquire the correct feel, the student will need an observer to start him on the correct hoof, after which he can continue until he has the correct feel.

The walk is a four-beat gait, each hoof landing separately, with an equal interval between each beat. The leg movement is laterally consecutive; i.e., after the right rear is grounded, the forehoof on the same side will be grounded, then the left rear will come to earth, followed by the left fore.

Due to the progressive walk cycle, the horse will variously have two and three legs in support at different times. There is a moment, as has been caught by the high speed camera, when the horse is in the apparently impossible position of being balanced on two legs on the same side.

A study of *The Horse In Action*, by Henry Wynmalen, will be

Walk, balanced on two lateral legs

immeasurably beneficial to any serious student of horsemanship and will clearly demonstrate the impossibility of precisely executing gallop departs from the walk unless the horse has the correct foot position.

Once the rider can clearly feel each beat of the walk, he must apply the gallop control after the forefoot that should lead the gallop has grounded and is moving back, and before the outside rear reaches the ground. The horse will have been given the necessary reaction time, and he will shove off with the outside rear. The inside fore, which just moved back, will swing forward and become the leading foreleg of the gallop.

But, of course, the horse must first be prepared for the command. All too often, we see a rider lost in concentration of the hoof sequence, riding the walk on a loose rein, suddenly apply the signal for a gallop, startling the unsuspecting horse into a wild instinctive leap in which he nearly falls. This is a classic violation of the rule, "Never surprise the horse," and always produces a nervous horse that attempts to anticipate the gallop command to avoid being surprised.

We prepare the horse by taking a firmer contact and placing him in second position. At the proper moment, i.e., when the feet are in the right place, we apply the gallop control with a slight lift of the inside rein and the oral command. In the beginning, we will allow the horse a few trot steps, until he learns the correct response to the rider's demand. Soon, by being patient and allowing the horse the necessary time, thus maintaining his calmness, we can teach him to do calm, supple, flawless gallop departs from the walk.

We began our gallop departs from the walk on a curved line in order to make it as easy as possible for the horse. As the horse gains in strength and ability, we will gradually straighten the curve until we are galloping from the walk on a straight line.

When galloping from a straight line of travel, we practice varying the leads to insure that our horse is responding to the controls and not, like a circus horse, taking his leads because of being turned.

The next step is to teach the horse the gallop depart from a stand-still. Gradually, before each gallop depart, we slow the walk until we are actually at a stop for a second or two before the gallop. By slowly increasing the length of time spent at the stop, we have taught the horse the necessary stationary collection for a standing gallop depart.

As all transitions from the gallop require the use of a half-halt, once our horse has developed the necessary strength in his haunches, as evidenced by the gallop departs from the spot, we must now begin work on full-halts from the gallop.

To prepare a horse for a full halt from the gallop, he must be placed in a *collected gallop*, not the *natural collected gallop* that is a natural gait of all normal horses, but the *acquired collected gallop* that is the result of gymnastic training. It is the gallop that only the horse with years of correct training can give his rider.

We begin, then, from the natural collected gallop and work toward acquired collection.

Our object in this work will be to slow the forward rate while maintaining the timing and the fresh springy action. Particular attention must be given that the three-beat gallop does not degenerate to a four-beat ruined gallop.

From the natural collected gallop, we accelerate the horse, lengthening the stride while maintaining the timing. The essence of this work will be in maintaining the timing (rhythm).

After the horse shoots forward for a few strides, we shorten the reins, in rhythm with the grounding of the rear hooves, simultaneously cautiously bracing the back in order to lightly load the haunches. This gathering in of the impulsion created by our legs, together with the loading back brace must be applied only during the first and beginning of the second phase of the movement, when the rear legs are grounded in support on bent hocks. This slight loading, through the reins and the seat, will cause the bent hocks to bend a bit more in support, gradually increasing their carrying capacity, and thus their ability for collection.

We repeat this action only for a few strides, shortening the length of stride only until the *original rate* of the natural collected gallop is reached, where we allow the horse to return to the natural collected gallop for a time before repeating the exercise.

In time, a small amount of collection may be retained throughout the movement and the horse not quite returned to the natural collected gallop. The slightly increased load through the seat, the rider sitting erect, and a back that is braced as needed to maintain the impulsion, with the assistance of the legs as needed, will keep the horse in a bit more of a collected carriage than the natural collected gallop.

Eventually, the horse will be capable of being pushed forward to the softly receiving hands, his collection being increased in one stride, with no increase in the forward rate, only increased action and elevation. In fact, the rate will eventually decrease as the stride is shortened, while the action and carrying capacity of the haunches is increased; i.e., the collection has been increased. But it is possible to increase the collection only by first eliciting a forward response to the rider's legs and back and then receiving this response and transferring the load to the engaged haunches.

When we have increased the collection at the gallop thus slowing the rate, we will apply a forward control at the moment the principal diagonal is grounded (second phase), causing the horse to engage his rear legs further under the load in the succeeding period of flight. As the rear legs are grounded again, we restrain the forward impulsion we have created by holding with our hands, continuing to press the horse to the bit with our legs and back, and stop the horse in the second phase of the gallop. Immediately our hands and forward controls relax, allowing the horse to return to a square stance. It would be a grave error to attempt to hold him in the initial position of the stop, for he would either fall heavily on the bit or step to the rear with his rear feet in order to relieve the overload on his hocks.

The transition from the collected gallop to the walk is very similar to the stop from the gallop, the difference being that before the horse is completely stopped, he is urged forward to a walk. His first step must be vigorous; he must not be allowed to drag or creep forward or fall heavily on the forehand.

The sequence of the transition is quite important, for the third gallop phase is almost identical to the corresponding phase of the walk, enabling the horse to make the transition easily. It also renders it impossible to effect this transition from any other gallop phase.

Now we can begin to practice the walk to gallop and gallop to walk transitions, the most beneficial gallop exercise known because of the affinity that it requires between horse and rider. As we work on these exercises, on an absolutely straight line, we will take different leads, but not alternate leads that would tend to routine the horse.

In conjunction with increasing the collection at the gallop, as previously described, we will begin work on the circle, the only exercise that is capable, through the mechanical loading effect of centrifugal force, of increasing the load on a single rear leg.

In this work, we will begin on a large circle and slowly decrease it, over a period of time—days or weeks, depending on the progress of the horse—to a volte (twenty-foot diameter circle). Care must be taken that the horse retains his collection (impulsion, timing, and

Counter gallop

action) and balance; and that he does not lean excessively into the turn and fall heavily on his inside foreleg. The rider's inside leg must remain vigilant and nip in the bud any tendency in this direction.

By working on the circle in both directions, increasing the load on the inside rear leg in each case, we will have increased, through strengthening each rear leg separately, the horse's ability for collection on a straight line.

When the horse can easily perform the volte at a collected gallop, we will begin work on the counter gallop or counter canter.

The counter gallop, called the wrong lead when performed without collection, is a gallop in which the lead is opposite to the direction of the turn. Or put another way, a horse that is following a curved line to the left will be leading with his right legs.

The purpose of the counter gallop is to teach the horse that he is not to change leads unless specifically ordered to do so (there are many horses that change leads automatically with a change of direction—and at no other time) and thus further refine the rider's control; increase the suppleness of the horse's loins through causing him to use muscles that he would not ordinarily use; increase the rider's control over the rear leg that was the outside leg and has now become the inside leg (the leg that constitutes the first gallop phase); through centrifugal force increase the load on the inside rear leg, the leg that, at the moment of landing, carries the entire weight of the horse.

Assuming counter gallop from a corner

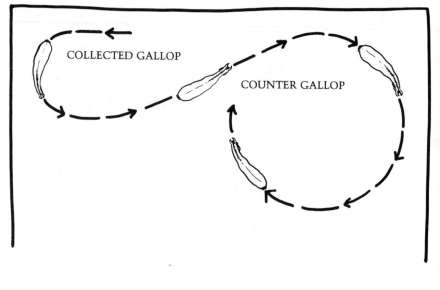

COLLECTED GALLOP

COUNTER GALLOP

COUNTER GALLOP   COLLECTED GALLOP

Assuming counter gallop through a flat serpentine

To perform the counter gallop, we place the horse in a collected gallop (a large arena is necessary for this work) down the long side of the arena. Upon reaching the corner we turn a large half circle and return to the wall, making the turn at the wall as flat as possible.

Another method of beginning a counter gallop is through a very flat serpentine down the center of the arena. We place our horse in the collected gallop on a slight curve to the left, then very gradually we turn to the right.

It is quite natural for the horse, following his instinct for preservation of equilibrium, to change his leads. The application of any disciplinary action for this change must be *unconditionally avoided* if future flying changes of lead are not to be made permanently difficult.

If any changes of lead are offered, gently—and the key word is "gently"—return to the walk until calmness is reestablished before resuming the gallop and again attempting a counter gallop.

In the counter gallop, the horse is flexed to the circumference of the arc of the circle, requiring a high degree of suppleness, especially on the volte; his outside leading legs are compelled to stretch further, thus increasing the horse's overall gymnastic ability.

In an absolutely correct counter lead although the horse's longitudinal flexion will circumscribe to the circle, the flexion of his lower jaw will be to the lead, in this case to the outside; i.e., he will remain *on the rein* on his leading leg's side.

37

Flying Change of Lead

When the horse can easily perform voltes at the counter lead in either direction, we will begin the work that reaches for the flying change of lead.

The flying change of lead is a natural movement for nearly all horses as evidenced by the fact that they are frequently seen performing faultless changes while running free in the pasture.

A flying change of lead is, then, a movement at the gallop in which a horse changes his leading legs, fore and hind, while in the fourth, or suspended, phase. It is, simply put, a gallop depart from the gallop, if we recognize that there exist two different gallops—a gallop with a left lead and a gallop with a right lead.

It is well to say, at this point, that there are sluggish horses who have not been endowed by nature with the gift of action and should not be tortured by attempts at flying changes of lead.

Our problem then, as always, is to cause a horse to perform a natural, simple movement when commanded to do so. We must first be able to tell the horse that which we want him to do, second, prepare him to do it, i.e., cause him to move in a state of collection that makes the movement possible, and third, have the horse sufficiently obedient so that he wants to do that which we ask.

At the risk of being repetitious (I would gladly be a bit tedious if it would prevent one trainer from trying to prematurely squeeze a flying change from a horse, producing a tense, *ears back* horse whose capacity for a calm, flying change is forever removed from his grasp), I must repeat emphatically that calmness is an *absolute requirement*, the number one priority, of work at the flying change of lead.

The gallop work we have been doing up to this point has been leading toward, among other things, a flying change of lead.

We begin our work by perfecting the simple change of lead. The simple change is done by changing from one lead to the other through a few strides of calm walk on a straight line. We will continue perfecting the simple changes until the horse can pass from the left collected gallop to two steps of a calm walk and back to a right gallop, gallop on for a short time and repeat the simple change from right to left.

When the horse can perform 100 simple changes, without a mistake, he is ready to attempt the flying change.

To clarify the rider's role in this cooperative movement, let's examine in slow motion, so to speak, the horse's movements during a natural flying change.

Our horse, while galloping, will enter the fourth phase of the gallop (suspended time) while leading with his left leg. He will be slightly flexed to his lead, following a straight line. He will land on his right rear leg (first phase); followed by his left rear and right fore (second phase, principal diagonal), and then, shifting his weight to the left rear, he will rock forward onto his left fore (third phase) and vault over it into the air. When he shifts his weight to the left rear, he shoves off strongly with this leg. *This is the moment in which the change is initiated.* In the air, this strong shove will effect a change of flexion to the right and cause the right legs to extend to accommodate this shove in their direction. The horse will then land on the left rear leg—the new first phase—followed by the right rear and left fore, second phase, and vault over his new leading right foreleg, third phase, and into the air. He will have changed his lead smoothly with no change of direction, loss of timing, or roughness, and he will certainly have remained perfectly calm.

This movement, this interchange of legs, that the horse has done by himself is what we wish him to do on command. Seem like a large order? Well, it is, and more trainers fail at teaching the flying change than at any other movement, because they fail to take the time to analyze, to "reduce to the lowest common denominator," the horse's action. They also hurry, and try to force a premature change before the horse is ready.

To effect a flying change while mounted with the horse's choreography for a flying change clearly in our mind, we ride down the center line of the arena at the collected gallop on the left lead. When we reach the center of the arena, we do a simple change of lead (through two steps of a calm walk). We repeat this a number of times to fix in the horse's mind the fact that we change the lead at exactly this spot. As horses become automatic and geographically trained very easily, we will use their natural tendency in this direction to make the first flying change as easy as possible.

After a few simple changes, we approach the "spot" at a collected gallop and begin to ask for a walk. The horse will engage his rear legs further under the load in order to comply. He will land on his right rear leg and immediately ground his left rear and right fore. At this moment, we must alter our seat, increasing the load on the left rear leg in order to make it the new dominant rear leg of support. After loading the left rear, we signal the horse to continue the gallop, causing him to shove off strongly with this new first-phase leg. As he goes into the air, we change his flexion, and he will reach forward with the right legs (as explained earlier, when a horse shoves off strongly with one leg, the other leg, or legs, will automatically take a longer step to accommodate the thrust) and land on the new first phase of the gallop (left rear) and continue on the right lead.

In our description of a correct flying change, we stated that the change must be done with no change of rate. This is certainly true concerning a deceleration, but in the initial changes, a slight acceleration is permissible to insure that the horse maintains the forward impulsion and shoves strongly into the stride wherein the change is made. After the horse becomes proficient at changes, this acceleration is converted to the increase of action that "jumps" the horse into the change with no alteration of rhythm.

After the change is made, we gallop on for a time before placing the horse in a free walk on a loose rein. We then return the horse to the stable, where he may think about this new development in the peace and contentment of his stall.

As soon as the horse understands the controls for the flying change, we cease to change on the "spot" and begin changing the leads at various places on the center line and on a diagonal line from corner to corner.

We can also introduce changes of lead from one curved line to another on a large circle (a more difficult movement, for a change of direction is involved). To do so we ride a few circles at the collected gallop, increase our collection as we approach the center of the arena, ask for a change, and continue riding on the contingent circle before changing to a walk on a free rein.

In a matter of days, the horse will have gained confidence in changing from a left circle to a right circle, and the exercise may be reversed, making a change from a right circle to a left circle. And when the horse progresses to the point where he is showing absolutely no nervousness or anticipation, changes may be made after *one* circle in each direction—a figure-of-eight.

Do not make the common mistake of repeatedly riding figures of eight, for the horse will soon become routined and attempt a change of lead each time a circle is ridden. In this respect, in order to refine our control, we will begin riding figures-of-eight on one lead; we will ride the counter lead on one circle of the figure-of-eight.

When the horse understands that he is to change his lead only when commanded to do so by the seat and legs of the rider, not by a change of direction or flexion, we will begin changes of lead from one counter lead circle to another.

In a matter of days, the horse will be able to counter lead a figure-of-eight with a flying change from the counter lead to counter lead at the spot where the circles are contingent.

We will now begin to *gradually* decrease the size of the circles, while riding these exercises, until they can be easily done with volte size circles. Then returning to flying changes of lead on the straight line of travel, we will begin to reduce the number of strides between changes.

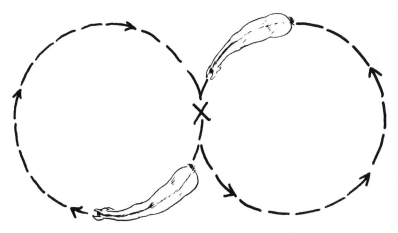

A flying change of lead from one large circle to another

The number of gallop strides necessary between flying changes will be one more than the smallest number of gallop strides that can be inserted in a calm walk. Or more simply put, when a horse can easily depart from a walk, complete five strides of the gallop, and return to a calm walk, he is ready for a flying change after six strides. When he can return to the walk after four gallop strides, he may do a flying change after five, and so on down the line.

When we have allowed the horse to gradually learn successive flying changes of lead after two gallop strides, we will attempt a change of lead at each stride, beginning on the left lead, changing to the right, and immediately changing to the left.

Before this point is reached, the horse and rider must be able to move as one unit, "cast in one piece," and the change of lead activated by a slight shift in the seat, a shift of weight from one seat bone to the other, and a thrusting forward of the hip on the side of the new lead. The horse-rider unity must have progressed to the point where the controls have become influences and the reins merely a means of thought transference between the two minds.

Strictly speaking, the change after two strides better demonstrates the horse's lead control, as one *pure* gallop stride is not possible between changes at every stride, although it is a requirement at the Grand Prix Olympic level.

Strict control over the number of changes done at each stride must be maintained by practicing a predetermined number—three, four, six, etc.—or the rider may find that he has "turned on" a change at each stride and is unable to "turn it off!" These multiple changes at one or two strides belong to the highly trained high-school level, and few are the horses with the natural ability to reach it. To complete the basic training of our horse, we should be content with flying changes after six strides on straight or curved lines.

38

Two-Track Work
at the Gallop

Two-track work at the gallop differs from that at the trot in that we now have the added complication of the leads, or changes of lead, with which to deal.

We begin by riding the collected gallop on a small circle in the corner before the long side of the arena. After a few circles, we ride down the long wall on one track. We repeat this a number of times, firmly placing in the horse's mind the fact that we will leave the circle by riding down the long wall. Now we circle and ride down the wall, but we do so just as the horse's head comes to the wall, on two-tracks, maintaining the flexion of the circle and the angle at which the horse came to the wall. Our lateral displacement will be such that the outside rear hoof will track the inside forehoof in "gallop position," called "gallop position" because "green" horses will often assume it naturally in their initial gallop training and also because of its similarity to second position, which is necessary for gallop training.

Upon reaching the corner, we return to one track and second position; the horse is not yet ready to travers a corner.

As soon as the horse is familiar with the left travers from the corner circle, we introduce the right travers from a circle in the opposite corner. In a short time, the circle will become unnecessary, and the travers may be assumed by merely riding through a corner

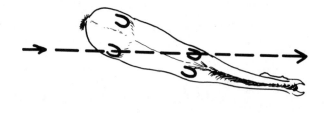

Gallop position: a slight travers with the outside hoof tracking the inside fore hoof

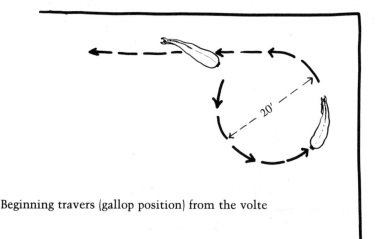

Beginning travers (gallop position) from the volte

at a collected gallop in second position, second position being easily translated to the gallop position as the horse's head comes to the wall.

At this level of training we introduce the gallop renvers in order to remove the psychological support of the wall. We ride down the long wall at a collected counter gallop, i.e., our left and lead side next to the wall. With our inside leg and both reins, we swing the horse's forehand away from the wall until the forehand has moved to the right one hoof width—the gallop position. We then introduce the same movement to the right.

Great care must be taken while entering the renvers that it is the forehand that moves away from the wall, not the haunches moving toward the wall in an effort to evade carrying its share of the load.

COUNTERLEAD

Assuming renvers left from the counter gallop

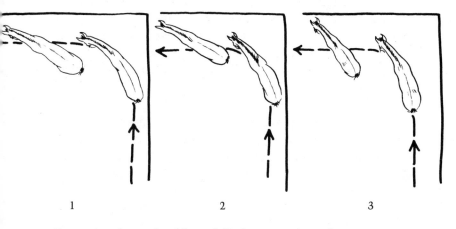

1   2   3

Increasing the angle of lateral displacement from the corner

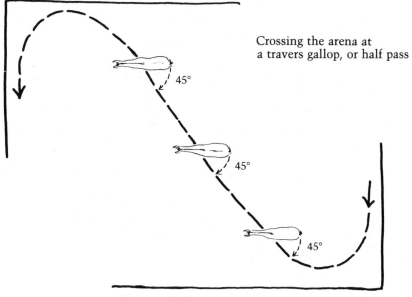

Crossing the arena at
a travers gallop, or half pass

45°

45°

45°

Returning to the travers, our natural line of progress lies in increasing the degree of lateral displacement. We accomplish this by beginning the movement at an ever increasing angle from the corner, or by entering the two-track movement sooner.

We continue to increase the angle of departure until we reach forty-five degrees from the line of travel.

In conjunction with this increased lateral displacement in the travers, the horse's angle of lateral displacement will be correspondingly increased at the renvers. He may now leave the moral support of the wall and traverse a diagonal line from corner to corner (that imaginary wall again)—in other words a half pass at a gallop.

The angle of lateral displacement from the line of travel will be the same as when we traversed the long wall (forty-five degrees).

When we reach the opposite long wall before the corner, we assume one-track and the counter gallop, in which we pass through the corner and around the arena. We do not ask for a flying lead change in order to prevent our horse from forming the habit of changing his lead upon coming to the wall. When our horse has become more accustomed to the half passes, we will vary a counter gallop with the flying change, always in such a way that he does not anticipate the change.

We will now begin to gradually increase the angle of lateral displacement by beginning the travers sooner, and at a greater angle, from the corner. We slowly increase the angle, providing the collection and impulsion remain constant, to fifty degrees, sixty degrees, seventy degrees, and, theoretically, to ninety degrees. I say theoretically because the forehand must continue to lead the haunches, even if only by an eighth of an inch, and even if only psychologically. The rider will feel if the haunches begin to lead, for the gallop will disintegrate to a four-beat ruined movement, and the fresh springy action will be lost.

After the horse has mastered the half pass it will be possible to perform a *full pass* from the center of one long wall to the other. As the horse is easily traversing at a ninety-degree angle to the line of travel, we merely move our line of travel from the corner to the center of the long wall.

Again, upon reaching the opposite wall, we will vary the counter gallop with a flying change of lead to prevent an automatic change of lead, offered by the horse and therefore out of control.

The horse should now be able to perform multiple diagonal changes of lead (zigzags) at the gallop, but before a change of lead and

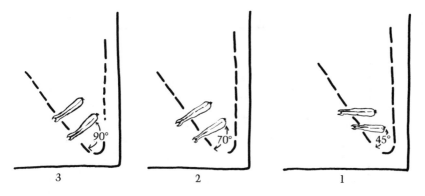

3 2 1

Increasing the angle of lateral displacement

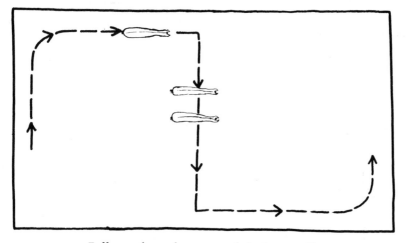

Full pass from the center of the long wall

a change of direction are simultaneously demanded, the horse, for a time, should be ridden straight forward for a few strides before being directed into a half pass in the opposite direction.

This is done to prevent anticipation in which the horse leans in the new direction of the half pass, thereby ruining the crispness and elegance of the movement. By gradually decreasing the number of strides between the changes of hand, the horse will finally come to perform multiple changes of hand at the gallop deviating three strides on each side of the center line.

The diagonal changes of hand at the gallop are very demanding on a horse, for he must simultaneously change his lateral and forward direction, his flexion, and his gallop lead.

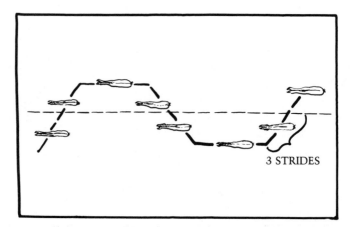

Teaching multiple diagonal changes of hand by traveling in a straight line between each change

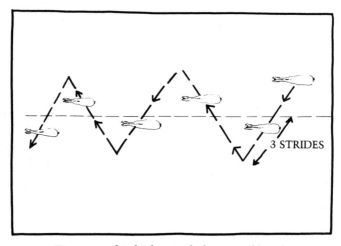

Zigzag: multiple diagonal changes of hand

PIROUETTE AT THE GALLOP

We will now begin the work of traversing curved lines, the work that will lead us to the pirouette at the gallop, but in order to eliminate confusion in the reader's mind, let's first take a look at the difference between the spin of a western stock, or reining horse, and the pirouette of a dressage horse.

A stock horse is trained to turn about, pivoting on his haunches, in order to herd cows successfully. He must be able to turn quickly, for some cows, especially calves, can move rapidly. He may throw himself around, leaning into the turn, as long as he turns at speed when directed to do so. The speed, in a sense, ruins his mobility, for he must come to a stop before moving forward. The spin is done more as a circus trick, in that, once triggered, it is difficult to stop, as evidenced by the fact that, at times, the champion stock horse goes off course in a competition by spinning an extra revolution before his rider can stop him.

The fact that the stock horse must stop his spin and gather himself before moving forward violates the rule of collection that says a collected horse must always be able to fluidly move forward without hesitating.

Another disadvantage of the spin of a western stock horse is the fact that he must throw his forelegs in the direction opposite the turn in order to maintain his balance upon stopping. He must move violently to avoid becoming unbalanced, thereby switching his lead.

This is not to say that all stock horses spin in this manner; there are those whose spin is more controlled, whose spin more closely resembles a pirouette. In fact, in these horses the line between a "spin" and a pirouette is at times difficult to draw.

In the above, I do not wish to detract from the justly won honors of the stock horse, a specialist in which more true collection will be found than in most others. I only wish to emphasize that, in the stock horse, too often balance, collection, and control are sacrificed for speed.

In the pirouette at the gallop, the horse enters the movement at a highly collected gallop, which is slowed to a gallop in place before the turn is begun. He does not lean into the turn, but remains perfectly balanced on all four legs (even loaded) and completes a 360° turn in four to six equal gallop strides, able at any stride to move forward in the same lead. And he completes the turn, or turns, at the same rhythm. The movement is done calmly, completely under control, demonstrating the highest degree of turn of which a horse is capable.

However, at the risk of disillusioning the reader and in order to paint a realistic picture, I must describe the pirouette that is too often seen in dressage competitions (even at the Grand Prix Olympic level).

The horse slows the gallop to a gallop in place at the indicated spot for the pirouette. The impulsion then dies, and the gallop de-

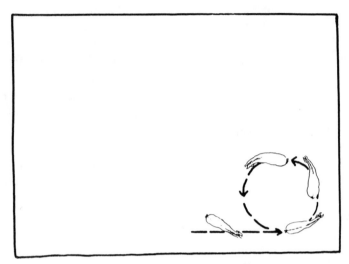

Traversing into a corner volte in a gallop position

Traversing a volte at a lateral displacement of approximately ninety degrees

generates to four beats; the horse throws himself about, like a seal, rear legs completely inactive, and completes the turn.

The stock horse aficionado sees this parody of a pirouette, gives out a derogatory "Huh!" and returns home, happy with his stock horse—and I don't blame him! At least his horse retains the priceless gift of animation!

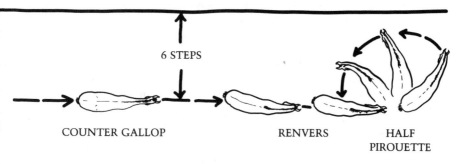

6 STEPS

COUNTER GALLOP   RENVERS   HALF
                                                    PIROUETTE

Teaching half pirouette in the corner

Once having understood the difference between a stock horse
spin and a pirouette, and the correct manner in which a pirouette
should be performed, we are ready to show our pupil. We begin
traversing curved lines by riding through the corner in *gallop position*, continuing the turn into a volte in the corner. Gradually, we
increase the degree of lateral displacement until we are traversing at
nearly ninety degrees to the line of travel on the circle. Our line of
progress now lies in reducing the size of the circle until the rear
hooves are galloping on the spot.

Not all horses are endowed with the powerful haunches and
loins necessary for learning the pirouette in this manner. A better
method for them is to counter gallop a parallel line approximately
six steps from the wall. Approaching the corner, we switch over to
a renvers gallop before traversing a tight circle in the corner. The
moral support of the corner wall helps the horse to understand the
required movement more easily.

In a short time the horse will be able to perform a half pirouette
in the corner, his rear hooves galloping on the spot.

When his loin, haunches, and rear legs have gained the necessary
strength, the half pirouette in the corner may be increased to a
three-quarter pirouette.

The rider should remember that, in all pirouettes, partial, whole
or multiple, the movement must be finished by riding straight forward at the gallop. He must feel that at any moment he could break
off the pirouette and continue straight ahead—if not, the pirouette
has gotten out of control.

After the three-quarter pirouette in the corner, the horse should
have no difficulty in performing a complete pirouette at any point

on the wall, and finally, as his proficiency grows, at any spot in the arena away from the walls.

The spirited horse, who in his overeagerness continually anticipates the turn into the pirouette, leaning into the turn, overloading his inside foreleg and losing his *even loading*, balance, and collection, must be slowed to a walk, and returned to the gallop only after the pirouette is completed. Being returned to the walk for the turn will soon restore his mental unconstraint, and he will be able to calmly gallop a pirouette.

If, after the pirouette, the collection of the gallop is improved, the rider will feel the increased suppleness and the greater bending of the hocks with each powerful elastic stride, the pirouette will have been done correctly and, more importantly, have had its desired effect of improving the horse's collection.

39
Backing

We have delayed the discussion of backing until now, not because it should not be introduced earlier in the horse's training, but because the time of its introduction will depend on the "feel" of the trainer.

If backing is taught too early in the training schedule, the horse will have learned a valuable weapon of defense, a weapon he will be all too ready to use when future training demands become difficult.

As a general rule, it is better not to introduce backing until the horse is *absolutely obedient to the forward control*—until he responds automatically to the forward control, without thinking and until forward impulsion has become a permanent acquired characteristic.

For example, a horse that does not want to go forward when ordered to do so will respond sluggishly to the forward control; and if this is allowed to continue, he will soon refuse to move forward, sticking to the spot. If this is not corrected, he will begin to back at any attempt to move him forward; and if the horse is not then corrected, he will begin to rear, and, finally, buck. He will always "progress" in this order.

A knowledgeable trainer will correct the lazy balky horse when he is in the first stage (sluggish response) by mercilessly riding him forward. He will not allow "holding back" to progress to a dangerous level.

A further example is a horse that, when first taught the turn on the forehand, will in order to disobey, move backward instead of stepping to the side with his rear legs. He will be using a learned response against his trainer.

By strategically introducing backing at an opportune moment, the trainer can avoid unnecessary problems.

In an attempt to answer the question that has perhaps risen in the reader's mind, "But if the horse will use everything I teach him against me, maybe I'd better not teach him so much?" I must emphasize that, along with teaching each movement, a rider must conjunctively teach the "stopping" of the respective movement. If he does not, he may find himself riding his horse at a trained racing gallop and belatedly discovering that he cannot turn it off.

Backing is not a natural movement for a horse. Unless he absolutely must move backward, he will swing his forehand around. Like the trot, the horse backs on diagonal legs, but without a period of suspension. The length of stride is limited, for the rear hoof remains grounded until the fore hoof on the same side has completed its stride (the grounded rear hoof always limits the stride of the fore hoof on the same side). Therefore, the rate of movement to the rear may only be increased by an increase in timing.

Backing work begins with the horse taking *one step* to the rear in response to a command. We begin, dismounted, by placing our horse beside a wall or fence as an aid in keeping the line of travel straight. We stand directly in front of the horse, facing him, our left hand on the lead, our right holding a crop by our leg. We take a step toward the horse, signalling him with an increase of pressure through the lead rein and the oral command, "Back."

By stepping toward the horse we have clearly indicated that we wish him to back out of our way. Most horses will understand and back one step, at which time we immediately pat them on the neck and speak to them in a rewarding tone.

If, for some reason, the horse does not step back, we maintain the rein pressure, repeat the oral command, and tap the horse on the chest (tap, do not strike!). After a few taps, the horse will take one step to the rear, after which he should be rewarded.

If the horse does not step to the rear, we will repeat the whole process, only this time we will continue to tap the horse's chest while repeating the oral command, tapping progressively harder until the tapping is definitely irritating to the horse, but never striking

Teaching the first step back

with enough force so as to elicit fear in the horse's mind. The tapping, when done correctly, will simulate the continual irritation of biting flies. We continue patiently in this manner until the horse decides to move away from the irritation. We must allow the horse the time to figure it out for himself. He can stand there and continue to be irritated, or he can step to the rear, at which time the irritation will cease immediately, and he will be rewarded, thus associating a refusal to step back at the oral and physical signal with discomfort and stepping back to the signal with comfort (a lack of discomfort being nearly equal to comfort).

In no case attempt to back the horse by forcefully shoving the bit. This type of shoving, besides pushing the horse back on his rear legs, making it impossible for him to step back, produces pain, fear, and stiffness and associates pain with the back command in the horse's mind. The fear-induced excitement impairs, as always, the horse's thinking ability. Backing a horse with a rein signal is called a "rein back"; the oral signal will eventually become unnecessary.

By progressing patiently, the horse will soon be able to take one, two, or any number of steps to the rear. The trainer must remember that he can ask for only one step with each signal; the hand and the oral command must pulsate in rhythm with the horse's steps.

After a few days of consistent schooling, the mounted rein back may be introduced to the horse—*if* he is backing perfectly straight, to a light rein and the oral command, while dismounted.

221

The safest way to begin is by riding a horse directly into a corner, the corner making it obviously clear that the horse must move back.

With the reins in our left hand, we lean forward, relieving the weight from the rear legs so that the horse may step back easily, place the crop before the horse's chest, apply a rein signal, and give the oral command.

In most cases, the horse will take a couple of steps back. If he does not, repeat the command, with voice and rein, and tap the horse's chest with the crop. If this fails, quickly dismount and back the horse from the corner.

It is not uncommon, as this is not a natural movement, for many horses to become confused at the first mounted rein back. Upon a refusal to rein back, we could easily force the horse to back by pulling strongly on the reins, or by striking his chest with the crop. The horse would rein back, but he would not rein back *calmly*! In fact, he would permanently associate a rein back with pain, thereby stiffening each time the rider even thinks *rein back*.

If, after dismounting and backing the horse from the corner a number of times, the horse still refuses to back, the aid of an assistant is necessary.

Teaching the rein back while mounted

The problem is one of transition; the horse learns to respond to a command in a certain situation, i.e., with the trainer dismounted, standing by his head. With the trainer mounted, the situation is changed, thereby confusing the horse. The horse needs a transitional learning period, which will be supplied by the trainer backing the horse with a mounted assistant. Now the situation has been changed, by the mounted assistant, but not so greatly, and the horse will understand.

As training progresses, the assistant will gradually take control, backed up by the trainer, until the trainer is no longer necessary. At this point, the trainer alone will have no trouble with a mounted rein back from the corner.

We must remember that we are not trying to prove our dominance over the horse (or perhaps our machismo). We are trying to teach him a calm rein back, one that will stay with him for the rest of his life.

When the horse is backing nicely from the corner, we will begin our backing progressively farther from the psychological support of the corner, until it is no longer necessary.

A rein back is not a forward movement—in fact, the horse is behind the bit—but it is an indispensable aid in training. Nevertheless, in order not to leave our horse behind the bit, we will always finish each rein back by riding forward a few steps. We will never rein back and stop.

It is well to mention, at this point, for it has been my experience that it is common and quite instinctive with many novice riders, that pulling on the reins and saying "Whoa" is not the correct way to stop a backing horse. The pulling on the bit only causes him to back more.

The proper way to stop a backing horse is by application of the forward control.

THE COLLECTED REIN BACK

In time, the horse will become proficient at the rein back; he will move calmly back at an imperceptible forward shift of the rider's weight and a touch of the rein, but he will move back with a high croup, stiff rear legs, and dragging forefeet—his backing education is by no means complete. He must be trained to back collectedly.

Introduction of collected backing must be delayed until the horse can easily maintain the trot with a definite degree of collection. He must first have learned collection at a forward gait. If he has not, the attempt at collected backing will probably produce only fear and confusion.

The collected rein back is taught as follows: Toward the end of a normal schooling session, liberally sprinkled with mounted rein backs, we stop the horse in the center of the arena. (It is important that there be no distracting influences present, for the horse will need his undivided concentration to *discover for himself* the proper response to the control we are about to apply.) We maintain our rein contact and gently signal the horse to go forward. When he raises a rear leg to step forward, we prevent him from doing so with the reins. The raised leg, prevented from stepping forward, will step to the rear. We lighten the rein pressure slightly, maintaining our forward control with a *passive back*, and the horse will continue to back. If we applied a strong forward-urging back control, we would stop the collected back and cause the horse to move forward without pausing; the horse must change the direction of movement fluidly.

It sounds much more simple than it is, for it requires a trainer with highly developed equestrian tact.

At the moment of restraint of the forward movement, the horse must discover, with no "clues" from the rider, that since he cannot go forward, and as he is being signaled to move, he must go in the only direction available: back. At this moment, the rider will be strongly tempted to "help the horse think" and rein him back. Any attempt in this direction will certainly move the horse back, but it will destroy any chance of the horse learning a *collected rein back*.

The horse must back because the forward impulsion, created by the forward control, is restrained by his obedience to the bit.

The rider must learn to use only the rein pressure needed to prevent the horse from moving forward (and of course the rein pressure must remain within the boundaries of bit obedience never degenerating to force). This means that once the horse begins to move back, only the lightest of rein contact will be necessary.

It is quite common, at this point, for riders to "cheat" themselves and make a rein back a good imitation of a collected back. The rider must be positive that he is not reining back. One sure proof of a collected back is the response to leg pressure—a horse that is backing collectedly will increase his rate to the rear. If he does not, he is being reined back. Another test of the *collected back*, as previously mentioned, is the fluid shift forward caused by bracing the back. The horse that is being reined back must stop and pause for a moment before moving forward.

A horse that is backing collectedly has the appearance of a collected horse. He is on the bit. His croup is lowered by the flexion and engagement of the rear legs and the load is relatively lifted from his forelegs, allowing them to step back freely.

The collected back is the basis of one of the frequently demanded high school dressage movements. This movement, called "The Rocker" consists of a repeated step forward and back, with no perceptible signal from the rider. "The Rocker," has been used as a requirement for entry in Olympic dressage competitions. It certainly is proof that the horse is collected and well under the influence of fine controls.

Backing collectedly may be used as an aid to increasing the horse's collection, for he cannot avoid coming to the bit with flexed and engaged haunches, flexing the joints of each rear leg as it comes forward, forced to carry a greater load on a bent hock as the other leg is lifted for a backward step. However, it can in no way cause collection.

As a disciplinary action, backing is an indispensable tool, for the horse that repeatedly bores on the bit, after repeated full halts, can be brought into hand (be made to come to the bit without stiffness) by collected backing.

As backing is difficult and always slightly distasteful to the horse, it should not be done indiscriminately. We should be satisfied when the ordinary saddle horse can back easily, and perfectly straight, for ten or fifteen feet.

40

Work at the Walk

Work at the walk began, informally, when we first led the horse forward. We were careful that our light reassuring contact on the lead rein did not interfere with the natural bobbing and weaving action of the horse's head, and thus cause a stiff, unnatural walk. We allowed the young horse to walk as he chose, adjusting our rate to his, as long as his steps did not become hasty or hurried, in which case our hand ceased to follow, and we held back, causing the horse to pull on our hand, until the relaxed elastic walk was reestablished. If this failed to regain the calm walk, we stopped and calmed the horse.

Then, as frequently happens, the horse, the newness of being led being somewhat worn off, began to slow and walk sloppily, dragging his feet; and we were forced to recapture the lost impulsion by introducing the "Come on" command, backed up by a touch of the training whip behind the hocks.

Thus we were able to insure that the young horse did not practice, and become habituated to the hurried or foot-dragging walk.

When the time was ripe, we introduced the horse to the lunge, using the previously taught accelerating command to prevent the walk from degenerating, and stopping the horse if he began to walk with hasty, tense steps.

As the horse's carriage and balance improved, through exercise at the trot and gallop, the improved carriage was automatically manifested in the walk.

At the beginning of mounted work, we did little with the walk, for we allowed the horse to carry the unaccustomed weight of the rider at the gait in which he was strongest, the trot. As the horse strengthens at the trot, he also becomes stronger at the walk, and now we are able to introduce the free walk.

The free walk is initially done on a completely loose rein that allows the horse complete freedom of the head and neck, so that the length of his stride and his free-swinging leg movement are not restricted. But he must walk vigorously, as if he were "going home." He should be immediately highly responsive to the rider's legs, which should swing with the movement and increase the pressure, almost accidentally, should the impulsion, freshness and vigor of the walk diminish. The rider must realize that all increases in rate must be done with an increase of the length of stride, with an active step, *but never with a hasty one.* When the rider's leg swings with the horse's barrel oscillation (applying a slight, momentary increase in pressure when necessary, in rhythm) the leg signal will be applied at precisely the correct moment: when the rear leg on the side of the leg signal is grounded.

The horse must not be prevented from slowing the walk, however irksome this continual urging him forward may be; for each

Free walk with light rein contact

Faulty conformation:
steep hocks

time the rider must "leg" the horse forward, the horse is learning to respond to a progressively lighter leg signal, and, eventually just the breath of a leg signal will restore the vigorous free walk. In time, the horse will learn to maintain an active free walk, rarely needing to be "legged" forward. Thus his action will be loose, free, and elastic.

When the long, roomy strides of the free walk—strides with regularity of length interval have been well ingrained in the horse, the rider may try, while at the walk, to pick up a light rein contact—with "glass-of-water wrists," a following hand that "breathes" with the horse's movement, and a rein that is in contact but not taut so that should the horse desire to stretch his neck a bit more, he would find the necessary slack. There should be just enough contact for the horse to "know" that contact has been, and is being, made.

There should be absolutely no visible change in the horse when rein contact is made. If there is a change, it is evidence that the horse, or the rider, is not ready for the free walk with rein contact. More free walking on a loose rein and work at the other gaits are needed before rein contact may be again attempted.

Work at the walk has been placed last in training for two reasons. First, it is the most difficult gait in which to train the horse requiring all of the finely graduated controls that a long period of training produces. Second, as the old truism states, "Trotting prepares for the gallop and the walk," and in order to achieve prowess at the walk, beyond the free walk, the horse's physical ability must be improved by a long period of work at the trot and gallop. If the horse's muscles and tendons are not changed (improved suppleness and strength), in much the same way as a ballerina's anatomical ability is changed by stretching and other exercises, it will be impossible for him to progress beyond the free walk to the ordinary, collected, or extended walk.

The horse, especially at the walk, cannot be trained beyond the limit of its conformation. The trainer will save himself much frustration and disappointment if he simply does not begin walk training with a horse with a short, straight rear leg, a leg that cannot "reach the ground" well ahead of the plumb line through the base of support of the haunches. The horse with steep, straight rear legs cannot take a normal walk step (one in which the rear hoof is grounded ahead of the corresponding print of its fore hoof), although he may be able to perform quite well at the trot and gallop.

After a time spent on the free walk, a time in which the gymnastic exercises in the natural and collected gaits have had time to take effect, the horse will be able to stretch a bit more and come onto the bit with absolutely no active movement of the rider's hands. In fact, any continual "nagging of the hands" in an attempt to present a false picture of a horse on the bit will prevent the horse from ever achieving the ordinary walk.

In the ordinary walk, the horse stretches forward to the bit as a result of lowered haunches and a greater engagement of the long-striding, driving rear legs. His load is thus being "evened-out" from front to rear and increasing his balance and poise, shortening slightly the stride of the rear legs to a small overreach of the fore-hoof prints.

It must be emphasized that, in this transition from the free walk to the ordinary walk, the rider's hands must remain passive. They must only sustain the increased rein pressure that the horse has placed on them by stretching forward, a stretching forward elicited by the rider's legs only.

It is true in all gaits, only more so at the walk, that the rider must have progressed to the point where he is able to sit and move supplely with the movements of the horse, his body in complete harmony with the motion of the gait, no cramps or stiffness interfering with the horse's supple movement, and able to apply the controls. In other words, the rider must be able to apply the controls without

Ordinary walk, with horse stretched onto bit

stiffening, while continuing to move as if he were part of the horse. This is the most difficult achievement in all riding.

The collected walk will naturally evolve from the ordinary walk as the rider gradually increases his demands and increases the engagement of the rear legs, causing the relative elevation of the forehand with a naturally rising neck—a neck that flexes more at the poll as it rises. Contact with the softly chewing mouth remains positive but soft as the rear legs increase their engagement on bent hocks, the horse entering the attentive ready state of collection, his maneuverability increased by his shortened base of support. The horse is mentally and physically ready to respond instantly to any command the rider gives.

In all work at the walk the rider must be sure that the hoof sequence remains that of a pure walk, and that the steps never become short through hastiness, tenseness, or rushing. The steps of the rear legs will shorten because of greater supple engagement on bent hocks until, in the collected walk, there is no overreach of the rear hooves. The rear hooves are grounded behind the print of the fore hooves.

The extended walk is possible after work at the collected trot. The rider then allows the horse to stretch, so to speak, letting the strides grow longer, the horse stretching further, reaching for the

yielding hand but retaining a degree of engagement of the haunches—
an engagement that now includes a stretching of stride until the rear
hooves far overreach the fore-hoof prints.

A horse that can go through the phases of the walk—from the
free walk to the ordinary, the collected, and the extended walks—
and return by the same route to the free walk, without his taking
one step of the trot or gallop, can be evaluated and his training said
to be correct.

41

Stationary
Collection

Stationary collection is a prerequisite to performing collected movements on one spot. It is the necessary preparation of the horse that insures that the movement will be executed flawlessly, for a stationary uncollected horse can only respond with natural (uncollected) gaits.

Let's take, for example, a gallop depart in the left lead from the spot.

We collect the horse, keeping him absolutely square, and, at the appropriate signal, he lifts into a gallop in the left lead, with no intervening walk or trot steps, for there must be no steps or shuffling about for a clean depart.

Now, if we attempt a gallop depart without first collecting the horse, he will not be in a physical position that would enable him to comply—and the gallop depart would always fail.

The horse, after having acquired balance and poise through a long period of gymnastic training, can shift his weight onto his rear legs without moving his hooves. Stationary collection must contain the three proofs of collection in motion: the horse must be ready, willing, and able.

One method, and perhaps the easiest, of teaching stationary collection, is through a series of gallop departs from the walk. The horse is first placed in a collected walk, the walk rate slowed a bit, before being asked to gallop. As training progresses, the horse will be slowed more and more, until he is actually stationary for a few seconds before being asked to gallop. Realizing that he will soon be asked to gallop, he will remain *ready*, and the stopping and sustaining of the *form* of the collected walk will have kept him *willing* and *able*. In due time, the rider will be able to stop the collected walk, without slowing, and hold the horse in a state of collection with a slight back control and light restraining rein.

Another method, is to introduce stationary collection from the collected back.

In the collected back, the horse is signaled forward and restrained while his rear hoof is raised to step forward, causing it to step back. In time, as the affinity between the horse and rider grows, the rider will be able to restrain the horse as he shifts his weight preparatory to raising his rear leg. He will be able to keep the horse framed in exact balance between the forward and restraining controls without moving the hooves. He will have placed a stationary horse in collection. The horse will then be able to directly enter any gait or movement that he formerly entered while in motion (collected trot, galloped pirouette, collected walk, etc.).

42

Introducing the Curb Bit

When a horse is capable of a definite degree of collection while standing on the spot and in all three gaits, when he is so well trained that strong rein actions are seldom necessary, when his flexions, especially at the ribs, are confirmed, the curb bit, with its indirect feathering action, may be introduced with the object of advancing the horse to even lighter bit responses.

As in all training advances, the horse will tell us, by resisting, through stiffness, going over, behind, or boring on the bit, if he is not yet ready for the loading action of a straight bar curb bit, a bit that, when it is accepted by the horse, simultaneously loads both rear legs.

A perceptive trainer, one who is not trying to prematurely present a picture of an advanced horse, will recognize the symptoms and will continue the training in the snaffle, postponing the curb bit work until a later date.

The horse must respond to the *signal* of the bit, and not to the *pain* it is capable of producing; for with the introduction of pain, unconstraint will be lost, and, with it, collection and any facisimile of horsemanship.

Due to the indirect action of the leverage bit (the shanks must be moved before an increase of pressure can be applied to the mouth), a slower increase of bit pressure is effected. This slower hand action further increases the horse's confidence in the rider's hands and permits a greater refinement of the controls.

We begin by fitting the horse with a light curb bit. A simple Weymouth will be satisfactory in most cases. The mouthpiece must be wide enough so that it will not pinch the corners of the mouth, leaving a quarter of an inch between the corners and the shanks. The mouthpiece should never be a narrow bar that will "cut in" or any other rough design that will create discomfort.

The shape of the horse's mouth will determine the height and width of the tongue port. For example, some horses have a "shallow" mouth in that the depth between the jaw bones is not deep enough to accommodate a large percentage of the tongue. Upon examination, it will be evident that a bit with a higher tongue port will be needed to bridge over the tongue and prevent excessive tongue pressure. Care must be taken that the higher port does not become high enough to press against the roof of the mouth when rotated. A discomfort of this sort, as found in the "spade bits," pries the mouth open and prevents a horse from ever coming to the bit unwillingly.

Of course, with a horse whose tongue is mostly sunken between the jaw bones, in a relaxed state, a low port will be satisfactory.

In addition to the snaffle in use at this stage of training—the size of the snaffle (rings and diameter of mouthpiece) may have been gradually decreased as the horse's training progressed—a separate bridle, fitted with the curb bit, is placed over the snaffle bridle, hence the name "double bridle."

Weymouth bit

Pinched corner caused by
a curb chain fastened too loosely

After the snaffle bit is properly adjusted so that it touches the corners of the mouth, the curb bridle must be adjusted so that the curb bit hangs below it, thus eliminating the possibility of pinching the tongue between the two bits.

It must not be hung so low that it rattles against the teeth. With a horse of normal jaw conformation, the curb bit will be in the correct position when its mouthpiece is opposite the curb chain groove.

During this critical introductory period, we should *not* attach the curb chain; we wish the horse to grow accustomed to the new bit *without leverage pressure.* We will definitely avoid the detrimental practice of leaving the curb chain excessively loose, for a loose curb chain is capable of pinching the corners of the mouth between itself and the mouthpiece.

The curb chain must be a flat wound chain that cannot cut in or chafe the curb chain groove. An excellent curb chain can be prepared by pulling the chain through a length of plastic tubing of the kind that can be found in most aquarium supply stores.

A chain is preferably to a leather curb, for the leather will continually stretch as it is wetted with saliva.

For the first few days after fitting the horse with the curb we will continue to ride completely on the snaffle rein, taking the slack from the curb rein only enough to prevent its swinging excessively. Gradually, as the days pass, we will begin to use the curb bit in conjunction with the snaffle, being constantly ready to return to the snaffle alone at the first sign of discomfort.

When the horse has grown accustomed to and has accepted the straight bar bit, we will attach the curb chain and adjust it correctly (*see photo of properly adjusted double bridle, page 10*).

Now we enter a truly critical stage of training, for the horse's mouth can either be *made* or *ruined* with the introduction of leverage.

So, very gently, and the accent is on gently, we pick up contact on the curb reins, in addition to the snaffle rein contact, in such a way that we do not frighten the horse into stiffening against the bit. We push the horse forward to the bit, and allow him to take contact on our hands, a contact which he chooses, for only the horse can know at which pressure he is comfortable.

We now repeat the complete mounted training program in the double bridle. Of course, this time we will progress through the training much more rapidly, and the horse will again learn the movements while accepting the double loading action of the curb bit. He will willingly accept the load that is simultaneously placed on each bent hock in true collection, with absolutely no use of force! All of his responses must be from a degree of obedience that allows him to remain supple.

Any loss of unconstraint, mental or physical, faulty flexion, over-bending or stiffness, or loss of the bold powerful elastic action, is proof that the preliminary snaffle work was faulty, and that the horse was placed in the curb bit prematurely.

43

Search for the Truth

And so we come to the end. I said earlier in this book that I would explain how to train a horse without arousing his undesirable involuntary reactions. I have now done so, and those of you who have stayed with me now have the theoretical knowledge of how to train your horse. Now comes the test, the putting into practice of the theory, the bending and the molding of the theory to fit the differences of each individual horse. The theory has flexibility that allows it to be adapted to each horse's personality, and this flexibility is what causes it to be the correct theory. Adapt the theory to fit the horse but never violate the principle goal of horsemanship: "Calm, forward, and straight."

The principle of horsemanship has been building for nearly twenty-four hundred years, since Xenophon, the ancient Greek general, wrote the first essay on horsemanship. Through the centuries the born horsemen, the equestrian geniuses of their time—men like François de la Guérinière, General L'Hotte and the great early maestros of the Spanish Riding School of Vienna, and, more recently, Colonel Alois Podhajsky and Waldemar Seunig—men who became legends in our time, have added to, strengthened, and bettered the principle of horsemanship.

We may change our methods of training to fit our environment and the individual horse of the moment, but when we change the principle we can never expect to achieve success. We are then, in effect, turning our backs on the great maestros of the past, men of a greatness who we can never hope to equal, men who gave their lives to the art of horsemanship.

The men who shine in the history of horsemanship have two things in common: their love of horses and the thirst for the truth.

To be successful we must also have a love of horses, but more than the love of watching horses in motion, at work or at play in the pasture, we must love the act, the time spent, of working and training the horse. And some of us will be wise enough to discover, one day, that although we long and strive toward the goal of a well-trained horse, the true joy and happiness was actually in the daily work and challenge of producing such a horse. Although we will certainly enjoy the finished horse, if there is such a thing, we will find a hollow spot in our lives when the job is done, and we will start another young horse to fill this hollow, vowing not to repeat the mistakes (and we *will* make mistakes) that we made while training the last one. And thus we will grow and mature as horsemen, the horses, as always, being our teachers. Then we will fully understand the title of Colonel Podhajsky's famous book, *My Horses, My Teachers.*

We must also have a thirst for the truth. We must never accept as a logical reason for a certain method, "My grandfather did it that way," or, "Because I said so," said in such a way as to imply: "I'm a far better rider than you, so do it the way I tell you," or, "I've always done it this way," or, "You don't know enough to be able to understand an explanation," or a long, vague explanation full of mysticism and double talk intended to confuse the novice.

All of these answers are given in an attempt to evade the question—because the person is ignorant of the truth or purposely intends to keep the truth his personal secret. A true horseman can always give a logical reason for that which he is doing with a horse at any moment. If he cannot, his training method is not based on logic.

Always ask your trainer or instructor why. For learning to do a certain thing without understanding *why you are doing it* is worthless.

Search for the truth, and when you find bits and particles of it here and there remember it and forget the rest. Slowly your treasure of truths will grow through hard work and experience (and an eye, ear, and mind that is always open for the truth), and when your treasure is large enough, you will consider yourself a competent horseman.

My purpose in writing this book was not to write a complete book of horse training, for that would require volumes, but merely to pass on some of the knowledge I have gained in forty years of working, always searching for the truth, with horses. I have tried to explain how the average person can improve his horse, as the title clearly states. The degree to which the horse owner wishes to improve his horse will, of course, depend on the satisfaction level of the owner. As for myself, I am never satisfied with the level of my horse's education and responsiveness. I am always striving for a greater degree of responsiveness, and as the old saying goes, "When the horse is as lightly responsive to the signal as possible, work at getting him lighter—until he will respond to the weight of the boot on the air."

This then, the constant improving of the horse, *is* the *art of horsemanship.*

Appendix

A TYPICAL SCHOOLING SESSION

As it has been necessary to insert explanatory subject matter in the chronological training order, and perhaps spread it so thinly as to lose continuity in the reader's mind, a description of the schooling session, at this point, is in order.

We begin the session by allowing, if possible, the horse to run about a large arena and buck out the kinks. If this is not possible, it will have to be done on the lunge, being careful to allow the horse as much freedom as possible (a forty-foot lunge line).

Some horses, when they are stiff and cold, will merely move about with short steps until they are "started"; then they will explode into action, and stretch their muscles.

After ten or fifteen minutes of free play, catch the horse and begin the lungeing work, working, at first, for an unconstrained trot.

When the horse has relaxed into the even timing of the unconstrained trot, his back muscles will be seen pulsating and his abdomen will oscillate from side to side, attempt a transition to the walk (with no loss of impulsion). Stay in the walk long enough to assure the horse that he has correctly understood before attempting the transition back to the trot. Do not change a horse quickly from one gait to another, as this tends to excite him. It is only the advanced horse that can make a string of rapid changes and remain calm.

When the horse is able to do acceptable transitions to the walk, obediently and smoothly, a gallop may be attempted to further relax

241

him. Be sure that the horse takes the correct lead and maintains a fluid three-beat gallop.

When the horse has been galloped enough (the perceptive trainer will know that the horse has become relaxed without being over-exerted), take the horse through the trot and walk to a stop, approach the horse and execute a half turn on the forehand, then repeat the above on the right hand.

Now that the horse is in the proper state of unconstraint, from having stretched and used his muscles and from the psychologically calming effect of obedience, we will try for some acceleration at the trot.

After the acceleration work, in both directions, we will saddle the horse and mount, being sure that the horse remains stationary, on a loose rein, while we mount.

As mounting is the rider's first association with the horse as a "rider," and as the horse *knows* that the rider wishes him to remain still while mounting, it becomes doubly important that the horse be made to obey and remain on the spot, *without being held*, while the rider mounts.

If the horse is allowed to be disobedient at the beginning of riding, *mounting*, then he can hardly be expected to be obedient during the mounted period.

The rule, never ride a horse before you can dominate him into remaining on the spot, on a loose rein, while mounting, must be rigidly followed if the horse's training under saddle is not to be seriously impaired.

After mounting, still on a loose rein, place the balls of the feet on the stirrup bars and stand vertically. When you are balanced, with no muscular action (pinched knees) necessary to maintain your position, relax your lower leg and allow your weight to lower your heels. Next, bend your knees and sink straight down to the seat. If your seat drops from one to two inches, your stirrup length is correct. This procedure is called "taking your seat" and is followed, and repeated, every twenty minutes or so by the greatest riders in the world, to reestablish the deep seat with the lowered heel.

Now that you are seated properly, pick up the reins, make contact with the horse's mouth, and wait a few seconds! We wait so the horse will not learn that rein contact means "Go forward." When we are sure that the horse is waiting attentively, without moving, we apply the forward control and walk forward.

If the horse moves with tense, nervous steps, we continue to walk until an unconstrained, free-swinging walk on a completely loose rein is achieved; then we pick up contact for a short time before placing the horse in a posting trot.

Being careful to post the inside diagonal and relieve the inside rear leg on the gentle curves through the corners, we try for a steady timing, followed by an unconstrained trot on a loose rein, and thus achieve balance and perhaps a degree of natural poise.

When this has been done in both directions, we ride to the center of the arena, dismount, and *lead* the horse from the ring. We *never* ride a horse from the arena, as we do not wish him to develop the ugly habit of speeding toward a gate, or slowing away from one. In this manner, the horse never expects to leave an arena while mounted.

Outside the arena, we mount, take our seat, and allow the horse the reward of rambling, in a relaxed manner, over the countryside.

We always walk the last mile or so of the return so that the horse does not get into the habit of rushing home, and also, so that he returns home well cooled out.

After off-saddling, we sponge off the back and girth groove with cold water and hose down the lower legs with cold tap water.

Do not brush where the saddle and girth were pressing. With the pressure of the saddle and girth, the capillaries (minute veins) are pressed shut, and circulation in the surrounding areas of the skin has been blocked. With the removal of pressure, the capillaries are greatly engorged with the sudden inflush of blood and are easily ruptured, causing bleeding in the skin and subsequent back problems. The cold water *gently* contracts these capillaries to normal.

The lower leg of the horse, the site of most lamenesses, must be cared for religiously *to prevent unnecessary lameness.*

The lower leg, from the knee or hock down, has no muscles, hence the blood cannot be returned by normal veinous action (muscles pushing on vein). In lieu of this veinous action, nature has equipped the horse with a sort of pump called the "second heart of the horse."

On the bearing surface of the hoof (the part that touches the ground) will be seen a rim (horn) about the edge, a white flaky sole area, and a piece of pie-shaped, hard, rubberlike, raised section called the frog. Sandwiched between the frog (in the hoof interior) and the last bone of the leg (coffin bone) is a spongelike material called the "Plantar Cushion."

When the horse places his weight on the ground, the Plantar

Cushion is compressed, pumping the blood up the veins.

In addition, the lateral expansion and contraction of the hoof itself contributes to the pumping action.

The evidence of hoof expansion and contraction may easily be seen on the bearing surface (hoof surface) of an old horseshoe at the heels. A shallow groove, concavity, has been worn in the iron by the movement of the horn.

After the "second heart" of the horse has pumped the blood from the hoof, the veins of the lower leg are left swollen and overfilled.

By running water on each leg for a few minutes, we are causing the veins to contract and return to normal, thus preventing a large percentage of future leg problems.

Index